THE MYSTERIOUS DISAPPEARANCE OF ROANOKE COLONY IN AMERICAN HISTORY

The In American History Series

IN AMERICAN HISTORY

THE MYSTERIOUS DISAPPEARANCE OF ROANOKE COLONY IN AMERICAN HISTORY

Zachary Kent

Enslow Publishers, Inc.

40 Industrial Road   PO Box 38
Box 398   Aldershot
Berkeley Heights, NJ 07922   Hants GU12 6BP
USA   UK

http://www.enslow.com

Library of Congress Cataloging-in-Publication Data

Kent, Zachary.
    The mysterious disappearance of Roanoke Colony in American history/ Zachary Kent.
        p. cm. — (In American history)
    Summary: Traces the dangers and adventures surrounding the short history of the first British colony in America, highlighting the roles played by Sir Walter Raleigh, Roanoke chief Wingina, and other individuals.
    Includes bibliographical references and index.
    ISBN 0-7660-2147-5
    1. Roanoke Colony—Juvenile literature. 2. Roanoke Island (N.C.)— History—16th century—Juvenile literature. [1. Roanoke Colony. 2. Roanoke Island (N.C.)—History—16th century.] I. Title. II. Series.
    F229.K44 2004
    975.6'175—dc21
                                                    2003011108

Printed in the United States of America

10 9 8 7 6 5 4 3 2 1

To Our Readers: We have done our best to make sure all Internet addresses in this book were active and appropriate when we went to press. However, the author and the publisher have no control over and assume no liability for the material available on those Internet sites or on other Web sites they may link to. Any comments or suggestions can be sent by e-mail to comments@enslow.com or to the address on the back cover.

Illustration Credits: Enslow Publishers, Inc., pp. 6, 25, 30, 37; Painting by Gilbert Stuart, reproduced from the *Dictionary of American Portraits*, published by Dover Publications, Inc., in 1967, p. 112; Reproduced from the Collections of the Library of Congress, pp. 9, 12, 13, 16, 19, 22, 28, 32, 41, 51, 54, 59, 62, 64, 74, 78, 81, 90, 95, 109, 110; Thomas Harriot, *A Briefe and True Report of the New Found Land of Virginia* (New York: Dover Publications, Inc., 1972), pp. 44, 46, 100.

Cover Illustration: Reproduced from the Collections of the Library of Congress.

★ CONTENTS ★

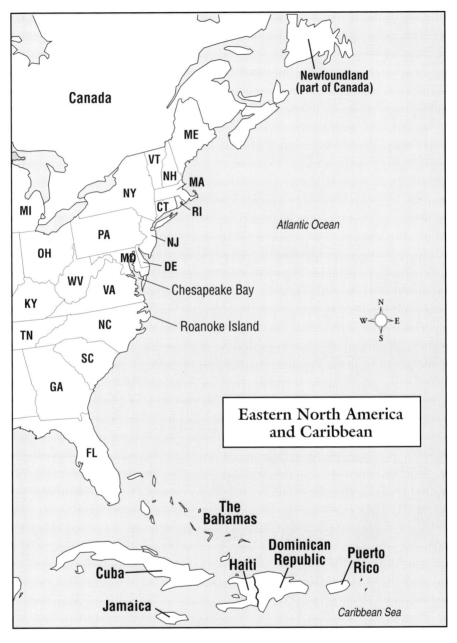

Newfoundland
(part of Canada)

Canada

ME
VT
NH
NY MA
CT
MI RI
PA
OH NJ
MD DE
WV
KY VA Chesapeake Bay
TN NC Roanoke Island
SC
GA

Atlantic Ocean

N
W E
S

**Eastern North America
and Caribbean**

FL

**The
Bahamas**

**Dominican
Republic** **Puerto
Rico**
Cuba **Haiti**

Jamaica Caribbean Sea

*Today, Roanoke Island is part of North Carolina in the
United States. During the time of the Roanoke colonists,
North Carolina was part of Virginia. The Spanish controlled
Cuba, Jamaica, Hispaniola (today Haiti and the
Dominican Republic), The Bahamas, Puerto Rico, and
Florida, as well as other parts of the New World.
Newfoundland was often frequented by European fishermen.*

CROATOAN

Eighteen Englishmen pulled at the oars of two longboats on August 17, 1590. The oars splashed in the water with a steady rhythm as the evening sun slowly sank in the west. At the stern of one of the boats sat John White, staring hard ahead across Pamlico Sound. White was hoping to see a sign of life on distant Roanoke Island. White was governor of a small English colony at Roanoke, along the coast of present-day North Carolina. He had been away for three long years. Now, on his return, he hoped to find a thriving colony.

A Night of Waiting

The longboats reached Roanoke Island after nightfall. In the darkness, they missed the usual landing place on the northern tip of the island by about a quarter of a mile.[1] The sailors had noticed the glow of a large fire in the island woods. They rowed in that direction.

Nearing the shore, the men dropped the anchors of the longboats. It would be dangerous to land in the darkness. Relations with the local Roanoke Indians were not good. So for their personal safety they anchored offshore. The sailors pulled in their oars, preparing to spend the night huddled in the boats.

Still, they hoped that the fire had been set by the colonists as a signal. White and the sailors shouted greetings and played songs on the trumpet that the colonists would have known. However, they got no response.[2] Uncertain of the cause of the fire, the Englishmen stayed in their boats. Through the night, White remained eager and full of hope.[3]

A Strange Clue

At dawn, the sailors rowed the longboats to shore and landed. They stepped through the woods toward the fire. When they reached it, White and the sailors discovered it was only the burning of some fallen, dead trees and fields of dry grass. Perhaps the fire had been caused by the intense summer heat. Perhaps it had been caused by lightning during a recent storm. It was clearly not a bonfire set by the colonists.

The puzzled men continued, searching for signs of human life. Governor White led the sailors along the shore. They walked toward the place where the colonists had been left three years before. Along the way, White thought he saw fresh American Indian footprints in the sand. "Round about the north point of the island . . . " White later explained, "we came to the place where I left our colony in the year [1587]."[4] The Englishmen climbed the sandy bank along a path that would lead them to the settlement.

Suddenly, they stopped in their tracks. A tree on the brow of the bank captured their attention. Into the bark of the tree, someone had carved "CRO" in large letters. It seemed whoever had begun cutting the letters had not finished the job. The meaning of "CRO" was a mystery the sailors could not solve.

An Empty Settlement

The men continued along the path until they reached the place where the English colony had been. The place was greatly changed since John White had been there last. White later wrote, " . . . their dwellings had been torn down and . . . a strong enclosure . . . like a fort, had been built."[5] One of the trees near the entrance of the fort had its bark stripped off. Five

When John White left Roanoke in 1587, the colonists were building a thriving settlement. When he returned in 1590, he could find no one. The settlement was deserted.

feet from the ground in capital letters the word "CROATOAN" was carved on the tree.

Governor White and the sailors entered the crude fort. They found some iron cannonballs and four rusty guns lying among the grass and weeds there. They left the fort and continued their search. They explored along the beach and up a nearby creek. They hoped to come across some of the settlers or at least their boats. However, they could not find anyone or anything.[6]

What was the meaning of the carved word CROATOAN? In 1587, 117 English settlers had landed in North America, hoping to establish happy lives for themselves. Just three years later, they had disappeared, leaving hardly a trace. Perhaps the carved word CROATOAN was left as a clue to the location of the people known today as "The Lost Colony of Roanoke."

THE NEW WORLD

Europeans first explored North America in about the year A.D. 1000. It was then that Leif Eriksson, a Norseman (from present-day Norway), briefly established a settlement. He called the settlement "Vinland." It was located somewhere along the coast of present-day Canada. The exact location is still uncertain today. Through the next five centuries, European sailors dreamed of finding a western sea route to Asia. They believed that the discovery of such a trade route would bring them riches. With such a route, the fabled gold, jewels, silks, and spices of China, Japan, and India would be more easily available to European traders.

The Rise of Spain

In 1492, Italian explorer Christopher Columbus bravely crossed the Atlantic Ocean in three small ships. The *Niña*, the *Pinta*, and the *Santa María* had been provided by King Ferdinand and Queen Isabella of Spain. On October 12, Columbus discovered land. He and his sailors stepped ashore on San Salvador. It was one of the small Bahama Islands in the Caribbean Sea. Columbus mistakenly believed that he had reached

Sailing under the Spanish flag, Italian explorer Christopher Columbus discovered the New World on October 12, 1492. The New World was "new" to the Europeans, but people had lived in the Caribbean, North America, and South America for thousands of years before Columbus arrived.

islands off the coast of Asia. He guessed that the riches of China, Japan, and India lay within his grasp. Therefore, as the friendly people of San Salvador pressed close around him, he called them "Indians."

Columbus had searched for a western route to Asia, but instead he had discovered an entirely new area of the world. Spain quickly took advantage of Columbus's discovery. During the next years, Spanish soldiers called *conquistadors* set out to explore the western half of the

On November 8, 1519, Hernán Cortes (sometimes spelled "Cortez") marched his soldiers into Tenochtitlan, capital of the Aztec Empire. The ancient city was located where Mexico City stands today.

world. Hernán Cortes conquered the Aztec Indian empire in present-day Mexico in 1519. By 1538, Francisco Pizarro had conquered the Incan empire located along the western coast of South America. These areas of the "New World" were rich in gold, silver, and spices. Soon, Spanish ships made regular voyages to bring these treasures back to Spain.

Sir Humphrey Gilbert

Many English people were jealous of Spain's growing wealth and power. England first successfully sent an explorer into the New World in 1497. Sailing under the English flag, Italian explorer John Cabot

SOURCE DOCUMENT

SIR: SINCE I KNOW THAT YOU WILL BE PLEASED AT THE GREAT VICTORY WITH WHICH OUR LORD HAS CROWNED MY VOYAGE, I WRITE THIS TO YOU, FROM WHICH YOU WILL LEARN HOW IN THIRTY-THREE DAYS I PASSED FROM THE CANARY ISLANDS TO THE INDIES, WITH THE FLEET WHICH THE . . . KING AND QUEEN . . . GAVE TO ME. THERE I FOUND MANY ISLANDS, FILLED WITH INNUMERABLE PEOPLE, AND I HAVE TAKEN POSSESSION OF THEM ALL FOR THEIR HIGHNESSES, DONE BY PROCLAMATION AND WITH THE ROYAL STANDARD [FLAG] UNFURLED. . . . TO THE FIRST ISLAND WHICH I FOUND I GAVE THE NAME "SAN SALVADOR."[1]

In 1493, after Columbus returned to Spain, he wrote a letter. (The recipient is not known.) In it, he described his amazing voyage of discovery.

(Giovanni Caboto) crossed the Atlantic Ocean. Cabot's ships touched upon the coast of Newfoundland, part of present-day Canada. Except for Florida and Mexico, all of North America at that time remained unexplored and unclaimed by Europeans.

In 1577, Sir Humphrey Gilbert made a daring suggestion to England's Queen Elizabeth I. Gilbert suggested that England establish a settlement in North America. From such a base, English "privateers" (pirate ships secretly supported by the English government) could capture Spanish treasure ships as they crossed the Caribbean Sea. In June 1578, Queen Elizabeth gave Gilbert the royal permission he wanted. He received an official charter. It was a document that stated that he was to "discover, search, find out, and view such remote heathen and barbarous lands, Countries and territories . . ." in the New World not already claimed by other European nations.[2] Gilbert promised Queen Elizabeth that he would establish a permanent colony in North America within six years.

Gilbert's first attempt began on September 26, 1578. It failed quickly due to storms that his ships encountered almost right away. He spent the next few years gathering another fleet of ships for a second voyage. They included the 120-ton flagship, the *Delight*, and the 200-ton *Ralegh*. The *Ralegh* was owned by Gilbert's younger half-brother, Walter Ralegh (sometimes spelled "Raleigh.") There were also three smaller ships, the *Golden Hind*, the *Swallow*, and the *Squirrel*. The five ships sailed from Plymouth, England, on

Though this picture shows many more men, John Cabot (standing and pointing) and only eighteen sailors landed their ship, the Matthew, *on the coast of Newfoundland in 1497. This became an important fishing area for Europeans. The drawing also shows John's son, Sebastian (to the left of his father); however, historians cannot confirm whether Sebastian made the voyage.*

June 11, 1583. However, just two days later, the *Ralegh's* crew discovered that they had not brought enough supplies. The *Ralegh* dropped out of the fleet and returned to port.

On August 3, Gilbert's remaining four ships reached St. John's Harbor, Newfoundland. For many years, European fishermen had been casting their nets in these waters. The fish they caught were mostly cod. The codfish of the region were becoming an important source of food to many Europeans. Gilbert found thirty-six Spanish, Portuguese, French, and English fishing boats anchored in the harbor. In a solemn ceremony, Gilbert formally claimed the harbor and all the land within six hundred miles of it for England.

Death in the Open Seas

During the voyage across the Atlantic Ocean, many of Gilbert's crew had fallen ill. Before continuing his explorations, Gilbert shipped the sick back to England aboard the *Swallow*. With his three remaining ships, he then sailed southward following the North American coastline.

Within days, dark clouds blackened the sky and fierce waves pounded the little fleet. The ships had sailed into a terrible storm. On August 29, 1583, the *Delight* ran aground in shallow water close to shore and sank. One hundred sailors drowned. The rough seas forced Gilbert's two remaining ships, the *Golden Hind* and the *Squirrel*, out into the middle of the Atlantic Ocean. On September 9, the rain poured down in torrents and the wind shrieked. Gilbert sat himself at the stern of the *Squirrel* and defiantly shouted, "We are as [near] to heaven by sea as by land."[3] That night, the *Squirrel* sank beneath the stormy ocean waves, drowning Gilbert and his entire crew. Sailing on alone, the *Golden Hind* reached Falmouth, England, on September 20, 1583. News of the tragic voyage soon reached Queen Elizabeth. Sir Humphrey Gilbert had failed to establish his promised colony in North America and he had died trying.

Queen Elizabeth's Favorite

Sir Humphrey Gilbert's younger half-brother, Walter Raleigh, wanted to make a success of Gilbert's mission. Tall and handsome, Raleigh was thirty years old in 1584. Raleigh was a clever, lively, educated man. At court, his striking appearance and quick wit had attracted the attention of Queen Elizabeth. According to legend, one day Raleigh spread his cape over a puddle so the queen would not get her feet muddy while entering her carriage. In those days of chivalry, that kind of noble, considerate behavior was greatly admired. Chivalry was the code of honor gentlemen and ladies followed.

In time, Raleigh became one of Queen Elizabeth's favorite courtiers. Courtiers were people who attended royal court. They presented themselves to the queen, often hoping for favors. Queen Elizabeth gave Raleigh large estates in England and Ireland. In addition, she granted him total control of England's wine and

During her reign, Queen Elizabeth I (1533–1603) strengthened England's role as a world power. While she was approving and overseeing Raleigh's expedition to the New World, the queen was dealing with her cousin Mary, queen of Scots, who was plotting to take the throne from Elizabeth.

woolen-cloth industries. Using his growing influence, Raleigh asked the queen for the right to take over Gilbert's charter.

On March 25, 1584, the queen granted Raleigh a charter. It was similar to the one she had issued to Sir Humphrey Gilbert. The charter gave Raleigh six years. During that time, he was to explore, settle, and claim as his own forever any lands not already discovered and occupied by Europeans. In payment, Queen Elizabeth would receive one-fifth of all the gold and silver that might be brought back to England. Both Walter Raleigh and Queen Elizabeth desired fame and fortune. They knew a successful claim of land in the New World could greatly benefit themselves and England.

AMADAS AND BARLOWE SET SAIL

A brisk wind snapped in the sails of two small ships as they left England on April 27, 1584. Captain Philip Amadas commanded the larger of the two ships. To assist Amadas, experienced Portuguese pilot Simon Ferdinando stood at the helm. Ferdinando had been to the Caribbean Sea before. As pilot, it would be his job to navigate the fleet. The smaller ship was a type called a pinnace. It was about thirty feet long. Captain Arthur Barlowe commanded it. Walter Raleigh had paid for the ships, and he had organized the voyage. Raleigh had ordered Captains Amadas and Barlowe to cross the Atlantic Ocean. They were ordered to search for a place to establish a North American colony.

The Outer Banks

From England, the two ships plowed forward through the salty, green Atlantic waves. They journeyed south to the Canary Islands, which are located far off the coast of Africa. They reached the Canaries on May 10. The sailors refilled the ships' water casks and then continued westward. On June 10, the two ships of

Before he financed Amandas and Barlowe's expedition to the New World, Sir Walter Raleigh (1554–1618) was a captain in the English Army, leading his troops at the siege of Smerwick in Ireland.

Amadas and Barlowe entered the Caribbean Sea. The sailors briefly landed on the Spanish island of Puerto Rico to collect more drinking water. Then, pilot Simon Ferdinando guided the two ships northwest to the Florida coast. This was a part of the world these English sailors had never experienced before. "The air smelt . . . as if we were in a fragrant flower garden," exclaimed Captain Barlowe.[1]

On July 4, 1584, lookouts stood high in the ships' rigging, the ropes that supported the masts. Suddenly, they shouted out that they had sighted land. It was the southern tip of the Outer Banks, off the coast of present-day North Carolina. These Outer Banks were long, sandy islands. They had been formed by the constant churning action of the ocean waves. The English ships sailed another 120 miles outside the banks. Finally, they arrived at a gap between two of the islands. The sailors wished to honor Simon Ferdinando, who had safely guided them there. They chose to call the place Port Ferdinando. On July 13, the two ships left the Atlantic Ocean behind. They carefully sailed through the gap at Port Ferdinando into Pamlico Sound. It was dangerous passing through the narrow gap. Even at high tide, it was only twelve feet deep.

Once inside Pamlico Sound, the sailors held a short religious service to give thanks for their safe arrival. They then rowed to shore and claimed the land for the queen of England.[2] The ship's longboats had landed on the Outer Banks island of Hatarask (present-day

Bodie Island). Not five miles away are the sandy dunes where Orville and Wilbur Wright would fly the first airplane at Kitty Hawk in 1903.

A Fine Report

One of Captain Barlowe's duties was to make a report for Walter Raleigh. Barlowe recorded many of the interesting things he saw during the voyage. "We . . . found the shores sandy and low toward the water's edge," Barlowe wrote, "and so overgrown with grapes that the surging waves flowed over them."[3]

Amadas, Barlowe, and their sailors walked inland to the nearby hills. Gazing about, they learned more about Hatarask Island. They discovered valleys of cedar trees beyond the hills and spotted some cranes (a type of bird).[4]

Hiking onward, the men discovered other sights. They spied deer, rabbits, and wild birds in great numbers. They walked through woods thick with pines, cedars, cypress, sassafras, and gum trees.[5]

Barlowe knew that Walter Raleigh would use his report to persuade Englishmen to invest in a permanent colony. Therefore, he made his descriptions as attractive as he could. "The soil," Barlowe declared, "is deep, sweet, healthy, and the most fruitful in the world."[6]

An American Indian Visitor

The English ships remained anchored off the coast of Hatarask Island for two full days. During that time, no

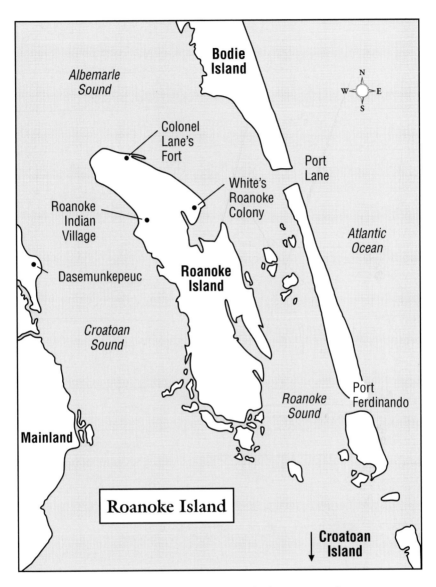

Roanoke Island

This is how Roanoke Island and the surrounding area appeared in the sixteenth century. Port Lane, Port Ferdinando, and parts of Roanoke Sound and the Atlantic Ocean have since filled in with land, making a solid strip of land to the east of Roanoke Island today. However other parts of the land have washed away, including the northern and southern tips of Roanoke Island.

American Indians were seen. But on the third day, three American Indians paddled near in a small canoe. They brought the canoe to shore, and one of the American Indians approached along the beach.

When Simon Ferdinando, Philip Amadas, Arthur Barlowe, and other Englishmen rowed to the beach and approached him, the American Indian delivered a speech of welcome in his language. "After he had spoken of many things not understood by us," Barlowe recorded, "we brought him . . . aboard the [ships]."[7] They presented the American Indian with a shirt, a hat, and some other small gifts. They also treated him to a dinner of meat and wine. The American Indian was given a friendly tour of both ships before being rowed back to land.

When the American Indian reached his canoe, he did not leave at once. Instead, he paddled into the sound and started fishing. In just half an hour, he filled the canoe with fish. Returning to the beach, he divided his catch into two equal piles. With hand gestures, he let the Englishmen know that his gift of fish was to be divided between the two ships' crews.

Granganimeo

The next morning, as many as fifty curious American Indians appeared on the shore. Their leader was Granganimeo, brother of the local chief, Wingina. Upon the beach, the American Indians spread a large woven mat on which Granganimeo and four other

American Indians seated themselves. The remaining Indians stood at a respectful distance.[8]

Amadas, Barlowe, and several sailors rowed to shore and landed on the beach. Granganimeo motioned for them to step forward and sit beside him. The American Indian leader then delivered a long speech. He made gestures that Barlowe recalled showed, "signs of joy and welcome, first striking his own head and breast and then ours, smiling and trying to show that we were all brothers, all made of the same flesh."[9] It seemed the English had established a friendly relationship with Wingina's tribe.

During the following days, dozens of American Indians visited the English ships. In exchange for deerskins, finely woven coral beads, and pots of colored dyes, the English traded such items as kettles, axes, and knives. Barlowe remembered, " . . . the thing that pleased [Granganimeo] most was a bright tin dish. He grabbed this, clapped it to his breast, and after making a hole in the edge he hung it around his neck, declaring with signs that this would shield him against his enemies' arrows."[10] For this single plate, Granganimeo gladly traded twenty deerskins. The American Indians thought a simple copper kettle was worth fifty deerskins. They would have given much more in trade for a sword. The American Indians were amazed at the sharpness of these strange weapons. But the Englishmen refused to make swords any part of their bargains.

Whenever the Englishmen fired a gun, Barlowe noticed the fearsome noise made the American

In July 1584, English sailors commanded by captains Philip Amadas and Arthur Barlowe successfully traded with the Algonquian Indians they encountered on the Outer Banks of present-day North Carolina. The expedition was funded by Sir Walter Raleigh.

Indians tremble. They had never seen or heard such an amazing thing before.

The Algonquian

The American Indians whom Barlowe and the others met were members of the general group called the Algonquian. The Algonquian occupied the coastal Atlantic region. The region extended from present-day Maine all the way to South Carolina. Like many other American Indian groups, the Algonquian of the North Carolina region were organized into tribes. Each tribe consisted of several villages of about one to two hundred people each. During the warm months of spring and summer, they lived on the islands in Pamlico Sound and on the islands of the Outer Banks. There, they fished and planted crops. The tribe of Granganimeo's brother, Wingina, lived on the nearby island of Roanoke in the summer. In the colder seasons, Wingina's people moved to the village of Dasemunkepeuc on the mainland.

These barefoot American Indians dressed in fringed deerskin skirts, which covered them from waist to knee. The men shaved their heads except for a ridge of hair down the middle. They often tattooed their faces and painted designs on their bodies. Pearl necklaces sometimes adorned their necks. Some of the American Indians wore copper earrings.

To feed themselves in the summer, these Indians gathered oysters, clams, mussels, and crabs in the shallow waters of the sound. They also fished with nets and

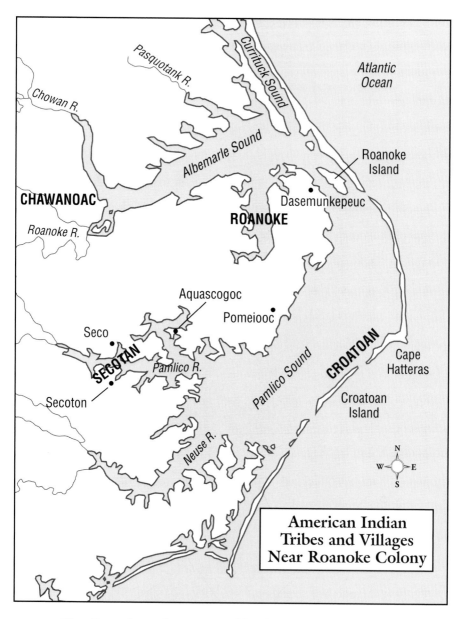

The Roanoke colonists would often visit neighboring
American Indians for help, to trade, to make peace, and
sometimes to make war. No matter the colonists' intentions,
American Indians often later suffered from European
diseases that they got during these visits.

spears and built weirs in which they caught fish. Weirs were traps made of woven reeds. These weirs were placed across streams and in shallow water. The traps were attached to the bottom by poles stuck into the sand. A well-built weir looked like a fence rising from the water.

The Algonquians were also expert canoe builders. They would select a thick, solid tree that had been blown down in a storm. Patiently, they scraped off the tree's bark with sharp shells. They then burned out the inside of the trunk with torches and gouged out the burned wood with their shells. "In this way," Barlowe remarked, "they fashion very fine boats and such as will transport twenty men."[11]

A Visit to Roanoke Island

One day, Captain Barlowe and seven sailors rowed a longboat several miles across Pamlico Sound. They wished to see Granganimeo's village on Roanoke Island. At the northern end of the island, they found Granganimeo's summer camp. It contained nine long-houses enclosed by a tall fence of wooden posts. The longhouses were built by inserting long poles of green wood in the ground at spaced distances. The poles were bent over to form a frame with a curved roof. The roof was then covered with woven mats of marsh reeds. Each house contained a wooden bench for sleeping. Outside, the American Indians cooked their meals over open fires in large clay pots.

Captain Barlowe and several sailors crossed Pamlico Sound in a longboat in order to visit Roanoke Island. They were greeted by the wife of Indian leader Granganimeo. In this picture, an Indian fish trap called a weir can be seen rising from the water in the foreground.

As Barlowe and his sailors rowed to shore, Granganimeo's wife ran down to the beach to greet them. She proved an excellent host, even though her husband was away from home.

Granganimeo's wife did all she could to see that her English guests were made comfortable. She led her visitors to a room in her large, five-room longhouse and asked them to sit by a fire.[12] The Englishmen were invited to remove their wet clothes. Several American Indian women took the clothes to wash and dry.

As Barlowe and his men rested, the women washed their feet.[13]

When they had dressed again in their dried clothes, the eight Englishmen were led into another room. There, they found plates of cooked venison (deer meat), fish, melons, and boiled vegetables prepared for them to eat. "We were entertained with all love and kindness," Barlowe marveled, "and with as much [food] as they could possibly [provide]. We found the people most gentle, loving, and faithful."[14]

After the feast, Granganimeo's wife urged her guests to stay in the village overnight. Barlowe and his sailors resisted, however. They preferred to sleep offshore in their boat. Granganimeo's wife was sorry that the English seemed to distrust the friendliness of her people. She sent about thirty of her people to guard Barlowe's boat.[15] During the night, rain began to fall. Some of the American Indians paddled canoes out to the longboat with "five mats to protect us from the rain . . ."[16] But the Englishmen still refused to return to the village. Barlowe later explained the reason. "There were only a few of us and we feared that if anything should happen the voyage would be endangered."[17] He made a point of adding, however, that he was certain there was no real cause for fear "for a more kind and loving people there can not be found in the world."[18]

End of the Voyage

For five weeks, the two English ships remained anchored in Pamlico Sound near Hatarask Island.

Finally, at the end of August, Amadas and Barlowe ordered the anchors raised. Captain Barlowe sailed his ship directly back to England. Captain Amadas, however, took a different route. Before heading home, Amadas first sailed north to explore the Chesapeake region. It was about one hundred twenty miles away. The Roanoke Indians had told the English that an excellent deepwater bay was located there. Sailing into Chesapeake Bay (off the coast of present-day Maryland and Virginia), Captain Amadas discovered fine places for ships to harbor. But when he landed men on shore, he discovered that the Chesapeake Indians were not nearly as friendly as the Roanoke had been.

Amadas set sail once more, and pilot Simon Ferdinando steered eastward into the Atlantic. The ship crossed the ocean through a terrible storm. In spite of the rough seas, the ship safely reached England near the end of September 1584.

Altogether, the voyage of Amadas and Barlowe had lasted nine months. They brought home exciting news of their adventures in North America. Walter Raleigh could use their valuable information to persuade Englishmen to invest in future voyages. "We brought home also," revealed Arthur Barlowe, "two of the Savages . . . whose names were Wanchese and Manteo."[19] Wanchese and Manteo were living proof that voyagers to the Outer Banks would be greeted by friendly American Indians.

The reports made by Amadas and Barlowe greatly pleased Walter Raleigh. Based on their new information, Raleigh immediately began planning for a permanent settlement in North America. He happily told English investors that his explorers had found a region of fertile soil. The place was also close to the

SIR RICHARD GRENVILLE'S EXPEDITION

Caribbean Sea. It could be used as a base from which to attack Spanish treasure ships on their way to Spain.

A New Knight at Court

Walter Raleigh was always a curious man who thirsted for knowledge. At home, he employed a personal tutor named Thomas Hariot. Hariot taught Raleigh science and mathematics. Now Raleigh asked Hariot to teach the American Indians, Wanchese and Manteo, English. At the same time, Hariot would try to learn the Algonquian language. To advertise his North American explorations, Raleigh dressed his American Indian guests in English clothes. He brought Wanchese and Manteo to London and introduced them at the royal court. Most of the English stared in wonder at the sight of them. They marveled at the appearance and behavior of Raleigh's very unusual, dark-skinned guests.

The results of Raleigh's expedition to North America impressed Queen Elizabeth. On January 6, 1585, she knighted Raleigh. She made Sir Walter Raleigh governor of the North American territory discovered by Amadas and Barlowe. It included much of present-day North Carolina and Virginia. Queen Elizabeth had never married. Because of this, she was known as "The Virgin Queen" of England. At Raleigh's request, she permitted him to call the new lands "Virginia" in her honor.

Assembling a Fleet

By the spring of 1585, Sir Walter Raleigh had organized a new fleet of six ships at Plymouth, England. On his next voyage, he planned to establish a permanent colony in Virginia. One of the ships was a Royal Navy ship provided by Queen Elizabeth. Raleigh provided three ships of his own. The other two were paid for by businessmen willing to invest in Raleigh's enterprise.

Raleigh boldly announced he would command this second expedition to North America himself. But Queen Elizabeth worried the voyage would be too dangerous. She refused to let her favorite nobleman leave England. So, Raleigh chose his forty-three-year-old cousin, Sir Richard Grenville, to take command. Altogether, Grenville's fleet would carry about six hundred sailors, soldiers, and colonists. The flagship of the

Sir Richard Grenville was Sir Walter Raleigh's cousin. He took over Raleigh's second expedition to North America when Queen Elizabeth refused to let Raleigh lead it himself.

fleet was the 90-foot, 160-ton *Tiger*. It was commanded by Grenville and piloted by Simon Ferdinando. The other ships included the 100-ton *Lion*, the 50-ton *Elizabeth*, the 50-ton *Dorothy*, the 14-ton *Roebuck*, and two smaller pinnaces.

Captain Philip Amadas received overall command of the sailors on the expedition. Lieutenant Colonel Ralph Lane would command the soldiers. The expedition also included a scientific research team. It was headed by Raleigh's personal tutor, Thomas Hariot. Joachim Ganz, a chemist, was hired as an expert in minerals. John White, a skilled artist, carried aboard watercolor paints and brushes. In those days before cameras, White was expected to make a record of whatever interesting things he saw. Other passengers probably included the kinds of craftsmen necessary to start a permanent colony, such as blacksmiths, carpenters, cooks, and bakers. The American Indians, Wanchese and Manteo, would return home on this voyage and act as interpreters for the English.

At the seaport docks of Plymouth, England, sailors carried supplies onto the ships. Casks of salted beef, barrels of warm beer, sacks of dried peas, and crates of hard biscuits were lowered into the ships' cargo holds. Barrels of gunpowder, brass cannons, pistols, and larger guns called "arquebuses" were also stowed away.

The Voyage to America

On April 9, 1585, Sir Richard Grenville's fleet at last weighed anchor and sailed out of Plymouth Harbor.

Just days at sea, a furious storm struck the fleet off the coast of Portugal. One of the pinnaces sank, and the entire fleet was scattered. Grenville ordered his flagship, the *Tiger*, to sail on alone. Pilot Simon Ferdinando set a course for the Caribbean Sea. During the next four weeks, the *Tiger* plowed ahead by itself through the foaming waves. The Atlantic Ocean voyage at last brought the *Tiger* to the Caribbean island of Dominica on May 7, 1585.

The sailors briefly rested on the island and collected casks of fresh water. Then, the *Tiger* sailed ahead to Mosquito Bay on the southwestern coast of the island of Puerto Rico. Mosquito Bay was the place where Grenville's captains had agreed to meet if the fleet got scattered. The *Tiger's* crew dropped anchor in the bay on May 12.

During his time in the Caribbean, the artist John White got out his paints and drawing materials. He drew pictures of many of the animals and plants he saw. Many of these animals and plants had never before been seen by Englishmen. White sketched and painted beautiful pictures of such creatures as a flying fish, a scorpion, an alligator, and a flamingo. He painted pictures of colorful flowers and even a pineapple.

While he waited for other ships to arrive, Grenville put his sailors to work. A replacement for the sunken pinnace was needed. On shore, sailors swung axes and felled trees for timber. Others sawed planks and set up a blacksmith's forge for making nails. Soon, a new pinnace began to take shape on the sandy beach. On

May 19, 1585, a lookout shouted out that he saw an approaching ship. The *Elizabeth* had successfully crossed the Atlantic and now joined the *Tiger* in Mosquito Bay.

The construction of the new pinnace was completed by May 24. The sailors aboard the *Tiger*, the *Elizabeth*, and the new pinnace hoisted their sails. The three ships glided out of Mosquito Bay. Heading north, the English ships happened upon two small Spanish ships, which they attacked and seized. The captured Spanish sailors soon revealed valuable information. There was a supply of salt, they told the English, piled on the beach at Salinas Bay, Puerto Rico.

Collecting Salt and Livestock

Sir Richard Grenville immediately ordered Colonel Lane, with sailors and soldiers, to take command of one of the captured ships. Lane was given the mission to collect the valuable salt. Salt was important because it was used to preserve meat and fish. At Salinas Bay, Lane's men constructed an earthen fort around the two large Spanish salt mounds they found there.

For three days, the men shoveled the salt into wooden barrels and loaded them aboard their ship. Then Lane returned to Grenville with his cargo of precious salt. At the same time, Grenville did some trading with Spaniards on Puerto Rico and Hispaniola. Hispaniola was the name of the island where the countries of Haiti and the Dominican

The forme of a fort wch was made by Mr Ralfe Lane in a parte of St Iohns Ilande neere Caprosf where we toke in falt the xxvjth of May. 1585

This is John White's drawing of the salt mounds on the beach at Salinas Bay. To protect themselves from Spanish attack, Colonel Lane's men built a fort around the mounds. Then they shoveled the salt into containers and carried them aboard their ship.

Republic are located today. Grenville obtained from the Spanish some pigs, cattle, and horses. This livestock would be valuable to his colonists.

On June 8, with these animals brought on board, Grenville ordered his ships northward through the Bahama Islands. On June 20, the voyagers sighted the coast of Florida. They reached their final goal four days later. It was a gap called Wococon on the Outer Banks of present-day North Carolina. Wococon was the inlet between Wococon and Croatoan islands.

At Wococon Inlet

Grenville's little fleet anchored off the Outer Banks at Wococon. It soon became clear, however, that the location was no place to establish a harbor. Pilot Simon Ferdinando tried to guide the *Tiger* through Wococon Inlet into Pamlico Sound. But pounding ocean waves drove the ship toward the shore. The rough water rushed back and forth through the narrow inlet. Too late, the sailors realized the gap was not deep enough. The *Tiger* was knocked repeatedly against the sandy bottom until the hull began to crack. Waves splashed across the ship's deck and flooded the cargo hold. Most of the colonists' food supplies were soaked and ruined. It was clear that large ships could not pass between Wococon and Croatoan islands into Pamlico Sound. The *Tiger* and the *Elizabeth* retreated several miles out to sea. In deeper water, the sailors dropped their ships' anchors. Grimly, Grenville and his officers discussed what they should do.

Within days of Grenville's arrival at Wococon Inlet, two more of his missing ships arrived at the Outer Banks, the *Roebuck* and the *Dorothy*. More good news soon came from nearby Hatarask Island. Three weeks earlier, Captain George Raymond aboard the *Lion* had arrived. Raymond had landed about thirty men on Hatarask before sailing on to Newfoundland. Now those thirty men joined Grenville's growing group.

In Pamlico Sound

While sailors repaired the damage to the *Tiger*, Grenville decided to explore Pamlico Sound. Taking the new pinnace and three longboats, Grenville set off on July 11 with about sixty men. The pinnace soon proved unable to sail in the shallow water. It was left behind. In the three longboats, Grenville and his explorers sailed ahead. Manteo served as guide and interpreter. The boats journeyed as far north as Lake Mattamuskeet and as far south as the mouth of the Neuse River. No Europeans had ever explored Pamlico Sound before. Grenville's longboats first reached the American Indian village of Pomeiooc on July 11.

Crowds of American Indians thronged the shore in greeting. "They are a people clothed with loose mantles [cloaks] made of deer skins," described Thomas Hariot, "& aprons of the same round about their middles. . . . And to confess a truth, I cannot remember that ever I saw a better or quieter people."[1] Artist John White made a drawing of Pomeiooc. It showed

Theodor de Bry's engraving of John White's drawing of Pomeiooc shows the high, protective wooden fence surrounding the American Indian village. Inside some of the longhouses, wooden sleeping benches can be seen. The villagers' temple is marked "A," the leader's house is marked "B," and a manmade pond for drinking water is marked "C."

eighteen longhouses enclosed by a protective fence of high wooden stakes.

On July 13, Grenville and his explorers left Pomeiooc and traveled forty miles up the Pamlico and Pungo rivers. Along the way, they visited the American Indian villages of Aquascogoc, Seco, and Secoton. John White's watercolor drawing of Secoton (an engraving of drawing is on p. 46) shows thirteen longhouses. Some of the longhouses reveal the sleeping benches inside. Elsewhere in the detailed drawing, two American Indians can be seen hunting with bows. Three fields of corn are growing in the picture, as well as other crops. Down and to the right, nine male dancers shake gourd rattles. More American Indians crouch on the ground nearby. At the center of the village picture, three American Indians sit eating boiled corn from wooden dishes set out on a woven mat.

In another picture, White drew the inside of a burial house of the village chiefs. The mummified bodies of the dead chiefs are shown laid out on a shelf.

Grenville and his men explored the region for a week. On July 18, the exploring party returned to Wococon Inlet. The brief journey had covered about two hundred miles altogether.

The Silver Cup

After leaving the village of Aquascogoc, Grenville's men discovered that the American Indians had stolen a silver cup from them. Two days later, Grenville ordered Philip Amadas to row back in a boat with eleven men.

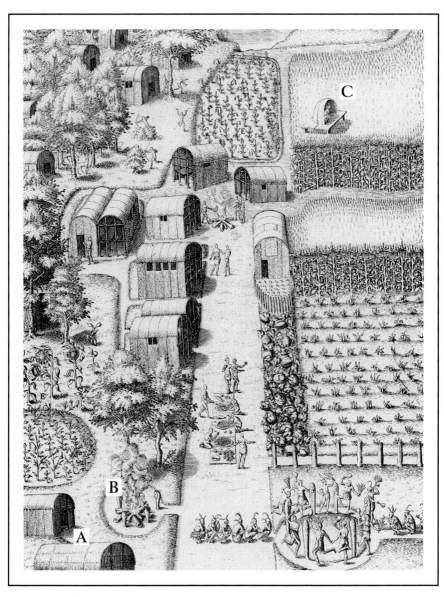

Many interesting details can be seen in Theodor de Bry's engraving of John White's drawing of the Indian village Secoton. A burial house for dead leaders is marked by "A," a fire reserved for religious rituals is marked by "B," a covered perch is marked by "C." From the covered perch, an American Indian would watch over crops so that they were not eaten by animals.

Amadas was sent to demand the cup's return. Amadas and his armed men soon landed at Aquascogoc. They found that all of the American Indians had fled into the woods.

Amadas decided to teach them a lesson. He ordered his men to set fire to the deserted village. They also torched the surrounding crops of corn. It was the first ugly conflict between the English settlers and the American Indians. The trusting relationship between the English and Aquascogoc tribe was ruined over a missing silver cup. By chance, the Aquascogoc were enemies of Wingina's Roanoke Indians. It is possible Wingina welcomed the news of the burning, when he later learned of it.[2]

A Settlement on Roanoke Island

By this time, the *Tiger* had been pumped dry and repaired. Three days after returning from his trip, Grenville ordered his sailors to raise their ships' anchors. The fleet sailed north from Wococon to the familiar inlet at Port Ferdinando. On July 29, 1585, Granganimeo climbed aboard the *Tiger*. Manteo stood beside him as interpreter. On behalf of Wingina, Granganimeo offered a place on Roanoke Island for an English settlement.

Having accepted a place to settle, the English knew there was a great deal of work to be done. Grenville's fleet of ships remained anchored in the Atlantic Ocean outside the sound. The distance to Roanoke Island through the inlet and across the sound was five miles.

Crates of supplies, tools, firearms, gunpowder, cannons, and live horses, cows, pigs, and chickens all had to be transferred. It required many trips by longboat in the August heat.

Once on the island, colonists swung axes and chopped down trees with which to build a fort. Acres of woods were cleared. The carpenters went to work with their saws, building gates and doors and making planks for floors. By the middle of August 1585, the wooden fort was finished. The colonists then began building simple cottages in which to live. Most likely, they were one-room houses with thatched roofs, containing perhaps wooden benches, tables, and bed frames. Probably the colonists constructed a blacksmith shop, a carpenter's shop, and a few storehouses, as well.[3] Their little village stood outside the walls of the fort, though it is uncertain exactly where.

On August 5, Grenville had sent one of his smaller ships back to England. He wanted John Arundell to carry news of the fleets' success at the Outer Banks to England as soon as possible. In time, Arundell arrived at court in London. Queen Elizabeth was delighted with the news he brought. In fact, she was so pleased that she knighted Grenville's messenger. He became Sir John Arundell of Tolverne.

Grenville's Promise

At Roanoke Island, the time arrived at last for Sir Richard Grenville to return to England. Colonel Ralph Lane and 108 colonists would stay behind. They would spend the winter in Virginia. During that time, Colonel Lane planned to explore the region. He would look for the best place to make a permanent settlement. Grenville left behind the little pinnace and several longboats for that purpose.

The sailors of Grenville's fleet at Port Ferdinando raised their ships' sails on August 26, 1585. Before leaving, Grenville promised Colonel Lane that he would be back by the spring of 1586. He would bring supplies, equipment, and more colonists. He told them he could be expected back by the Easter holiday. The *Tiger* then sailed away from the Outer Banks.

The last ship of the fleet, the *Roebuck*, set sail around September 8. It soon disappeared over the eastern horizon of the ocean. Colonel Ralph Lane and his fellow colonists realized that they must now survive on their own in North America. Surrounded by American Indians who they hoped would remain friendly, they faced an uncertain future. They also stayed on constant lookout for Spanish ships that might pass along the coast and attack them. With luck, they hoped to remain safe and healthy until the spring.

RALPH LANE IN COMMAND

Colonel Ralph Lane did not forget his duty. He would seek a better location for an English settlement, one with a good, deep harbor for ships. He would also try to discover if gold or other valuable resources could be found in the vast, untamed land of Virginia.

Early Discoveries

In the autumn of 1585, Colonel Lane sent an exploring party northward up the coast, bound for Chesapeake Bay. When they got there, the Englishmen quickly realized it was a broad bay with deep water. Surely, it would provide a far better harbor than any other place along the Outer Banks. Lane's explorers returned to Roanoke in February with their news. Until Grenville returned to Roanoke, however, with more supplies and men, a move to Chesapeake Bay could not be made.

At their little settlement on Roanoke Island, the colonists had the sheep, pigs, and cattle they had brought along for food. They could fish in Pamlico Sound and hunt for deer on Roanoke Island. But it

Thomas Hariot and John White studied the habits of the American Indians. They planned to make a report to Sir Walter Raleigh when they returned to England. In this picture, White shows an American Indian canoe and different ways the Indians caught fish.

was too late in the year to plant crops. To help feed the colonists, Wingina generously gave them baskets of corn and other foods.

Thomas Hariot learned how the American Indians grew their corn and wrote about the method in his journal. In the spring, the American Indian men and women worked in their cornfields together, removing weeds, grass, and old cornstalks. Then they poked holes in the ground and planted the seeds. Bending low, they spaced the seeds about an inch apart. They then covered them with small mounds of soil. Between the corn mounds, they sometimes planted beans and peas whose vines grew up the cornstalks. The American Indians also grew potatoes, melons, gourds, pumpkins, and sunflowers. The Algonquian added to their diet whatever nature offered. In the woods, they picked wild fruit and berries and gathered nuts in season. With their bows and arrows, they killed deer, bear, and other wild animals for meat.

One American Indian crop especially interested Hariot. "Uppowoc" was a leafy plant grown in carefully tended plots near their longhouses. At harvest time, the Indians picked the leaves and dried them. Then they crushed them into rough powder. According to Hariot, the powder was then smoked in a pipe.[1] Often Hariot joined the Indians in smoking "Uppowoc." He added in his notes that it was called "tobacco" by Spanish people.[2] The Indians believed that tobacco was healthful. They thought the smoke cleansed the head and chest. Hariot soon greatly enjoyed the smoking habit himself. Sadly, when he returned to England, Thomas Hariot became the first recorded case of a constant tobacco smoker to develop cancer. Hariot would die of cancer of the nose.[3]

Searching for Treasure

Wingina's people provided Lane's colonists with enough food to survive the winter. They gave the Englishmen corn, venison (deer meat), fish, oysters, and mussels. The American Indians collected the lovely round pearls they sometimes found inside oysters and mussels. They gladly traded these pearls to the colonists. Hariot described that "one of our company, a man of skill in such matters, had gathered together from among the savage people about 5000."[4] The man

SOURCE DOCUMENT

AFTER GOLD AND SILVER WAS NOT SOON FOUND, [THEY] HAD LITTLE CARE FOR ANY OTHER THING BUT TO PAMPER THEIR BELLIES. SOME ALSO WERE OF A NICE BRINGING UP, ONLY IN CITIES OR TOWNS. . . . BECAUSE THERE WERE NOT TO BE FOUND ANY ENGLISH CITIES, NOR SUCH FAIR HOUSES, NOR . . . THEIR OLD [FAMILIAR ENGLISH] FOOD, NOR ANY SOFT BEDS OF DOWN OR FEATHERS, [VIRGINIA] WAS TO THEM MISERABLE.[5]

A number of Ralph Lane's colonists were gentlemen adventurers. Their only interest in Virginia was to find gold or other precious minerals. In his report, Thomas Hariot expressed his low opinion of these Englishmen.

made a necklace of the best pearls. He planned to present the necklace to Queen Elizabeth as a gift when he returned to England.

It was clear that the English were very excited about pearls. So the Roanoke Indians told them that more pearls could be found among the American Indians living to the north. As a result, early in November 1585, Colonel Lane sent an expedition northward in the direction of Chesapeake Bay. This was the land of the Chesapeake Indians in present-day Virginia. The English explorers journeyed along

During the winter of 1585–1586, the English searched for gold and other treasure at American Indian villages. Many of the men with Colonel Ralph Lane were adventurers. They had come to North America hoping to make themselves rich.

the shore and fifteen miles up the Elizabeth River. They traveled as far as Skicoac, the largest village of the Chesapeake.

Spreading Disease

At the same time, between September 1585 and March 1586, Colonel Lane sent exploring parties to visit American Indian villages along Pamlico Sound. The English probably traded knives, tools, colored cloth, and pieces of copper.[6] In exchange, they received enough corn to keep them fed through the winter.

It did not take long after the Englishmen visited some American Indian villages, before Indians began dying. No one understood why. Thomas Hariot noticed this was especially true at villages where the English had not been fully welcomed. Within "a few days after our departure from every such town," declared Hariot, "the people began to die very fast, and many in short space; in some towns about twenty, in some forty, in some sixty. . . . The disease was so strange, that they neither knew what it was, nor how to cure it."[7]

Although they did not realize it, Grenville's men were spreading disease. In the 1500s, no one understood how germs were passed from person to person. The English carried such European diseases as smallpox and measles without even knowing it. They spread the germs of their diseases by coughing and sneezing and touching with dirty hands. The American Indians had no resistance to these germs. They had never been exposed to them before. Even the common cold, which could lead to pneumonia, was a sickness powerful enough to kill them. The American Indians decided the deadly illnesses they suffered were the result of a strange and mighty power of the English. "They were persuaded that it was the work of our God . . . " recorded Hariot, "and that we by Him might kill . . . whom we would without weapons, and not come near them."[8]

Among the Chawanoac Indians

Around the beginning of March 1586, Wingina told Colonel Lane disturbing news. Wingina claimed that Menatonon, chief of the Chawanoac Indians, was planning an attack on the colonists. Lane decided he must to something. He loaded soldiers aboard the pinnace and two longboats. They sailed into Albemarle Sound and up the Chowan River to Chawanoac. Without warning, Lane burst into the Chawanoac village with his men. The surprise of some forty Englishmen, dressed in armor and carrying guns and swords, stunned the Chawanoac.

Lane seized and handcuffed Menatonon, chief of the Chawanoac. Menatonon was an old man, paralyzed in the legs. He could not defend himself. During the next two days, the frightened Chawanoac chief told the Englishmen whatever they wanted to hear. He described a powerful American Indian nation to the northeast. It was called Chaunis Temoatan. Menatonon said it was rich with pearls and gold. Lane decided to take Menatonon's son, Skiko, as a hostage. With Skiko as a prisoner, Lane felt sure the Chawanoac would not dare attack the English settlement. Lane sent the pinnace back to Roanoke Island, with Skiko under guard.

The Search for Chaunis Temoatan

With the rest of his men, Colonel Lane set off in search of Chaunis Temoatan. About thirty armed men, crowded in two longboats, began rowing up the Roanoke River. They brought with them two large English hunting dogs of the breed called mastiffs. They knew the American Indians were usually frightened by these dogs.

Lane and his men rowed mile after mile upriver, fighting the river current. Sometimes they spied campfires along the shore. But each time they landed, they discovered that the American Indians had fled, leaving no food behind. The Englishmen soon realized that they were in real danger of running out of food. Lane called a halt. "I willed them to deliberate all night upon the matter," he reported.[9] The next morning, the men voted on what to do. Lane later declared, "Their resolution wholly and fully was . . . that while there was left one half pint of corn for a man, that we should not leave the search of that River."[10]

The tired and hungry explorers continued rowing against the Roanoke River current. That day, they heard American Indian shouts from the woods along the riverbank. Manteo, who was traveling with the

English, insisted these were war cries. As the leading longboat turned toward the shore, arrows suddenly whizzed through the air. Arrows struck the boats and glanced off the armor vests the Englishmen wore. But no one was injured in the attack. The Englishmen fired their guns into the trees. They landed on shore, ready to fight. But by then, the American Indians had retreated into the woods.

Lane established a strong camp on the riverbank. In three days, he and his men had traveled about one hundred miles upriver. They had not found Chaunis Temoatan. Their food was gone, and they were desperate for something to eat. That night, they butchered the two mastiff dogs and roasted them over the fire for supper. They flavored the roasted dog meat with sassafras leaves. The next day, the exhausted explorers agreed to return to Roanoke Island. As the morning sun rose in the sky, the two longboats glided in the river current back to Pamlico Sound. They reached Roanoke Island the day after Easter Sunday.

Hard Times At Roanoke

Sir Richard Grenville and his supply ships had not arrived by Easter, as promised. His failure to return caused hardships for the colonists. The Roanoke Indians suffered, too. The Englishmen pressured them to provide more and more food, but the Roanoke had enough work to do to feed themselves. Wingina ordered weirs set up in the shallow waters around Roanoke Island for the colonists to use. Thomas

This is John White's drawing of a typical Roanoke Indian. It is unknown if it is a picture of Granganimeo, Wingina, or some other warrior.

Hariot also noted that "in the end of April he had sowed a good quantity of ground [with corn. It was enough] to have fed our whole company . . . for a whole year."[11] Besides that, Wingina set aside land for the Englishmen to farm themselves. But, unfortunately, it would be several months before harvest time.

In the meantime, Lane decided to follow an old American Indian custom. He sent some of his men away to feed themselves on distant islands until the corn crop was ready. Twenty men under Captain Edward Stafford sailed to Croatoan Island, thirty miles to the south. Ten more were carried in the pinnace to Hatarask Island.

The friendliness of the Roanoke Indians gradually lessened with each passing day. Wingina's people could not provide enough food to support so many Englishmen. The colonists expected baskets of corn during the very months when the Roanoke Indians themselves usually went short. To add to the growing tension, Granganimeo had died that winter. Without his brother to advise him, Wingina behaved in a less friendly manner toward the Englishmen. Finally, Wingina deserted the American Indian village on Roanoke Island. He ordered his people back to their mainland village of Dasemunkepeuc.

The Death of Wingina

Ralph Lane became convinced that Wingina was planning war. Lane believed Wingina would soon attack the English settlement with the help of neighboring

American Indian tribes. Lane reported that the captured Chawanoac Indian, Skiko, had given him details of Wingina's plans. Colonel Lane decided to strike first. Lane sent word to Wingina that he intended to visit Dasemunkepeuc.

On June 1, 1586, the English colonel landed at the village. He found Wingina seated on a mat talking with other American Indians. Suddenly, Lane shouted his signal for attack: "Christ our victory."[12] By shouting this, he signaled his hope that their faith in Jesus Christ would bring the English victory. Dozens of his soldiers, who were hidden in the woods, quickly opened fire. As the guns roared, the surprised American Indians ran in all directions. Wingina fell to the ground, as if dead. But in another moment, he jumped to his feet and ran into the woods.

Lane handed his pistol to his Irish servant, who fired. The bullet wounded Wingina in the buttocks, but still he ran forward. Several soldiers with swords chased after the American Indian chief. They caught up with him among the trees. Before long, another Irishman, Edward Nugent, returned to Lane. He carried Wingina's bloody, decapitated head in his hands. It was a gruesome death for the Roanoke chief. His people would not forget it. Never again would the English have a good relationship with the Roanoke Indians.

In June 1586, Admiral Sir Francis Drake brought a fleet of ships to Port Ferdinando on the Outer Banks near the Roanoke Colony.

It was June 8, 1586, just one week after the bloody attack on Dasemunkepeuc. On that day, Captain Stafford on Croatoan Island sighted the large white sails of an approaching fleet. The twenty-three ships were commanded by English Admiral Sir Francis Drake.

SIR FRANCIS DRAKE

Drake was England's greatest living naval hero. As an explorer, Drake had been the first Englishman to reach the Pacific Ocean in 1578. He had been the first European to explore the Pacific coast of Canada. Aboard his ship, the *Golden Hind*, Drake, in fact, had been the first English sailor to circle the globe completely.

War with Spain

It seems strange that farming conditions in Spain should have had an effect on the English colonists at Roanoke. But that is what happened. In 1585, the kingdom of Spain suffered a dangerous food shortage. Farmers had had little rain and a bad harvest. The Spanish people faced starvation unless they obtained a supply of grain. On May 19, 1585, the Spanish King, Philip II, solved the problem. Spain was a Catholic nation. The Spanish viewed the English, who were Protestants, as religious enemies, anyway. Now King Philip seized every English grain ship anchored in Spanish ports. That sudden action marked the beginning of a war between England and Spain.

The English fleet that Captain Stafford spied off the coast of Croatoan had left England in September 1585. For almost a year, Admiral Drake had been attacking Spanish settlements in the Caribbean Sea. Drake's sailors looted the Spanish cities of Santo Domingo in Hispaniola and Cartagena on the coast of

England was at war with Spain in the fall of 1585. In the Caribbean Sea, naval hero Sir Francis Drake attacked several Spanish settlements, including the town of Cartagena shown here.

present-day Venezuela. Then, Drake ordered his ships to steer northward. The English naval force soon reached the coast of Florida. There, Drake attacked and destroyed the Spanish fort and town of St. Augustine in June 1586. The attack was so complete that the English even carried away the iron locks and bolts from gates and doors. Those items could be reused later. One week after they left St. Augustine, Captain Stafford sighted the English fleet as it cruised outside the Outer Banks. In response, Stafford had his hungry men light signal fires on the beach. Admiral Drake ordered longboats lowered, and contact was soon made.

Lane and Drake Make Plans

Sir Francis Drake told Captain Stafford that he was bringing supplies to the Roanoke colonists. He announced that he would sail his fleet up the coast and anchor off Port Ferdinando. Stafford hurried by long-boat back to Roanoke Island with his thrilling report.

Drake's fleet arrived at Port Ferdinando on June 11. It anchored in the deep ocean water two miles outside the Outer Banks. Lane soon arrived to greet the famed admiral. He climbed aboard Drake's flag-ship, the *Elizabeth Bonaventure*.

The two men exchanged their news. Drake was dis-appointed that Grenville's supply ships had failed to arrive. He learned that the colony was short of food and worried about American Indian attacks. The two men reached a compromise. Drake would give Lane two pinnaces and several other small boats from his fleet. More important, he promised to leave the ship *Francis* there until August. It was hoped that Grenville's supply ships would arrive by then. If they did not, Lane was to explore Chesapeake Bay in the *Francis* before returning to England. During the next few days, the *Francis* was to be filled with enough supplies to last the colony for four months.

A Fateful Storm

On June 13, a number of Lane's colonists boarded the *Francis*. They were there to assist in the transfer of supplies into its cargo hold. The journal kept by Drake described what unexpectedly happened next: "there arose a great storm that lasted three days together, and put all our Fleet in great danger."[1] A witness aboard one of Drake's ships declared that the winds rose up along with "thunder and rain with hailstones as big as hens' eggs. There were great [water] spouts at the seas as though heaven and earth would have met."[2]

As the terrible hurricane raged, the English captains did what they could to save their ships. Drake's four largest ships sailed away in search of deeper, calmer waters. When the skies at last cleared on June 16, Admiral Drake discovered the *Francis* had disappeared. Ralph Lane's promised supplies, as well as a number of his colonists, were gone. In addition, many of the smaller boats promised to the colonists had been sunk or wrecked against the shores.

Drake surveyed the damage to his fleet. Generously, he offered the colonists a second ship, the *Bark Bonner*. But the storm had greatly shaken the spirits of the Roanoke colonists. Lane and his officers worried that Grenville's supply ships were lost at sea. They guessed that the ships never would arrive. Colonel Lane now reached a speedy decision. Instead of remaining at Roanoke, all the colonists would return to England with Drake's fleet.

The colonists packed their possessions in a hurry. Manteo chose to go with Lane, and so did another American Indian, Towaye. They had become loyal friends to the English. When leaving Roanoke Island, the pinnace carrying the colonists ran aground in shallow water. To lighten the load and refloat the ship, many chests and crates were thrown overboard. Thomas Hariot and John White later made a grim discovery. Chests containing many of their journals and drawings had been tossed into the water. The pearl necklace intended for Queen Elizabeth was also accidentally lost. The haste to leave Virginia was so great, three of Lane's soldiers were left behind. Perhaps they had gone off on a hunting trip, but they could not be found in time.

The remains of Drake's fleet, with Lane's colonists on board, weighed anchor on June 18, 1586. They started the voyage home. The English ships sailed first to Newfoundland, where they took on fresh water and a supply of cod. Then, they crossed the North Atlantic and reached Portsmouth, England, at the end of July.

Too Late to Help

By a twist of fate, just two weeks after Lane abandoned Roanoke, Sir Richard Grenville's supply ships reached the Outer Banks. Grenville had left England in late April 1586 with eight ships. In August, the fleet anchored off Port Ferdinando. Grenville boarded a longboat and ordered his sailors to row for Roanoke Island.

Grenville and his men found the Roanoke settlement deserted, except for a gruesome sight. The body of one colonist, perhaps one of the three left behind, lay rotting on the ground. Another corpse, the body of an American Indian, swung by a rope from a tree. The Englishmen never discovered how these deaths had happened.

There were no Roanoke Indians living on the island. They remained camped at Dasemunkepeuc. In his ships, Grenville carried a year's supply of food and four hundred men. Grenville was unwilling to leave the Roanoke settlement completely abandoned. But strangely he decided to leave only fifteen men behind. He sailed away from Virginia in the third week of August. He later explained, "After some time spent in seeking our Colony . . . and not finding them [the expedition] returned [to] England."[3] Grenville and his fleet arrived back in England on December 26, 1586.

Ralph Lane's Accomplishments

During his ten-month stay on Roanoke Island, Colonel Ralph Lane had left a bad impression on the region's

American Indians. He had pressured them to support his colonists with more food than they could easily give. The English had accidentally spread deadly diseases among the American Indians. Lane's soldiers had savagely attacked American Indian villages and had beheaded the Roanoke chief, Wingina. These were brutal memories the American Indians would not forget.

Sir Walter Raleigh was probably upset when Lane and his men returned to England in July 1586.[4] Lane's failure to establish a permanent colony left many English investors doubtful about Virginia. Raleigh turned to Thomas Hariot for information he could use to promote future colonization. Hariot provided his employer with his notes describing the American Indians' habits and resources. Hariot's report described the natural life of the area in glowing terms. And John White's detailed watercolor pictures supported Hariot's claims.

Both Colonel Lane and Thomas Hariot reported that copper and perhaps gold could be found in Virginia. Certainly pearls could be collected. Also, Hariot brought tobacco and the smoking habit back to England. Hariot's enthusiasm for tobacco led Sir Walter Raleigh to introduce smoking at the royal court as the latest fashion. Raleigh still hoped to make his investment in the New World a success. But he realized Virginia would never make money unless a permanent colony were established.

7

RETURN TO ROANOKE

For three years, Sir Walter Raleigh had raised money and prepared ships. In spite of his hard work, he seemed no closer to his goal. There was still no permanent colony in North America. With the return of Colonel Ralph Lane and Sir Richard Grenville, Raleigh had to make a decision. Should he try again to make a settlement or should he quit Roanoke altogether and bring Grenville's fifteen men home?

John White Goes to Work

Raleigh was a busy man and was losing interest in his colonial adventure. The artist, John White, however, had been to Roanoke twice. White remained very enthusiastic about Virginia. In January 1587, Raleigh encouraged White to organize a land corporation. A corporation is a group of people united together to govern a town or city. White's land corporation would be called "The City of Raleigh in Virginia."[1] White and a council of twelve assistants would govern the corporation. The corporation would handle details Raleigh had no time to deal with himself. Raleigh and White began planning another expedition.

Raleigh decided that, this time, he would not depend on soldiers and adventurers to populate the colony. He would rely instead on volunteer investors—families determined to develop the land themselves. The corporation offered five hundred acres of land to any family willing to settle in Virginia. It was decided that the colonists would not settle on Roanoke Island. Instead, a new settlement would be established in Chesapeake Bay.

John White arranged for a fleet of three ships to take the colonists across the ocean. He searched the city of London and neighboring towns for volunteer settlers. He called for hardy men willing to bring their wives and children across the wide Atlantic Ocean to the wilderness of North America. White's own list of the colonists suggests that fourteen families, as well as other people, finally signed up. The list included 91 men, 17 women, and 9 boys and girls for a total of 117 people.[2] Each of the English families bravely invested their own savings for five hundred acres of Virginia land. A farm of five hundred acres was considered a large one in England at that time. John White remained so enthusiastic he persuaded his own daughter, Eleanor, to join the expedition. She would come with her husband, Ananias Dare, a brickmaker. White convinced his daughter to take the risk, even though she was pregnant.

The three ships organized for Raleigh's new expedition included the 120-ton *Lion*, with Simon Ferdinando again as pilot. The second ship was of the type called a flyboat. The third was a smaller pinnace. When all was ready, the little fleet set sail from Plymouth, England, on May 8, 1587.

Strangers in a Strange Land

From the very start of the voyage, John White and Simon Ferdinando did not get along. On May 16, the rudder of the flyboat broke. White complained when Ferdinando chose to leave the damaged flyboat behind in the Bay of Portugal. Ferdinando was too impatient to wait for the ship to be repaired.

Forty-two days of sailing later, the two remaining ships reached the Caribbean Sea. On June 22, 1587, the *Lion* and the pinnace dropped anchor at St. Croix in the Virgin Islands. The colonists stared about in wonder. The bright blue sea and the swaying palm trees of this strange new land amazed them. It was all so different from everything they had ever known in England. Rowed to shore, the colonists examined the island with innocent curiosity. Some colonists picked a fruit that looked like a small green apple. Hungrily, they bit into the wild food, but soon spit their mouthfuls out. They discovered that the fruit was poisonous. John White later described that, for about a day, their mouths and tongues burned and swelled.[3]

Several other colonists carelessly drank from a pond of stagnant water. The water proved to be foul. The faces of those who washed in it swelled so much that their eyes stayed closed for five or six days. Luckily, a search party found a spring of clear, fresh water to drink. They also captured five giant tortoises to eat. The strange beasts were so big sixteen men could barely lift one.[4]

At the Mercy of Simon Ferdinando

It seemed to John White that Simon Ferdinando and his sailors were more interested in privateering than in transporting colonists. After leaving St. Croix, the Portuguese pilot ordered the two ships to cruise among the Caribbean Islands for the next three weeks. Ferdinando hoped to capture Spanish treasure ships, but none were ever seen. John White urged him constantly to fulfill his duty and bring the colonists to Virginia. At last, Ferdinando steered northward. On July 22, 1587, the *Lion* and the pinnace finally arrived off the Outer Banks and anchored near Port Ferdinando.

It was White's plan to make contact with the fifteen men left the summer before by Grenville. Then, the ships would continue north along the coast to their final goal, Chesapeake Bay. Simon Ferdinando, however, had a different plan. He waited until White and forty of the colonists had gathered aboard the pinnace. They were about to leave on their visit to Roanoke Island. Then, one of Ferdinando's followers suddenly called out from the deck of the *Lion*. He loudly instructed the sailors on the pinnace not to bring any of the forty colonists back again. They were to be left at Roanoke. Only White and a few of his assistants would be allowed back on board the *Lion*. The excuse

Ferdinando gave was that "the Summer was far spent."[5] It was already too late in the year to sail on to Chesapeake Bay. It seemed to White, however, that Ferdinando and all the sailors only wanted to return to the Caribbean Sea to hunt for Spanish treasure ships.

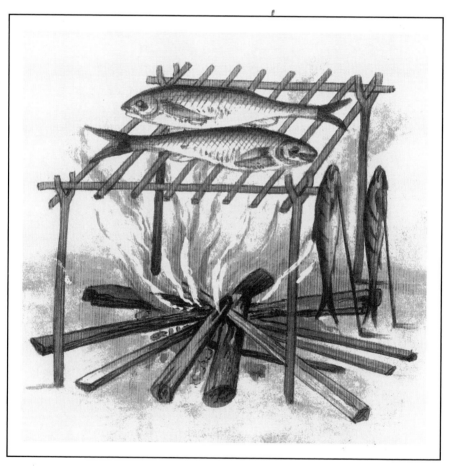

Another picture drawn by John White shows how the American Indians he met grilled their fish. When White returned to Roanoke in 1587, he discovered that the Indians had abandoned the island altogether.

Although stunned by Ferdinando's decision, White and his fellow colonists continued in the pinnace to Roanoke Island. They landed and searched for Grenville's fifteen men, but White had another disappointment. No sign of the missing men was found. However, they did find one colonist's bones. Apparently, White and the others thought that this person had been killed by American Indians.[6]

A Settlement at Roanoke

Early the next morning, July 23, White and his colonists continued their search. White recorded in his journal that he and several others "walked to the north end of the island, where Master Ralph Lane had his fort . . . where we hoped to find some signs, or certain knowledge, of our fifteen men."[7] They walked through the woods until they reached the settlement. There, they quickly saw that the high wooden fence surrounding the fort had fallen into ruin. All the cottages still stood. But no one had lived in them for some time. Melon vines were growing up through the clay floors. The Englishmen surprised some deer that were nibbling on these greens. No evidence of Grenville's colonists could be found.

Because Simon Ferdinando was determined to leave them there, Governor White had little choice. "The same day order was given," White explained, "that every man should be employed for repairing of those houses, which we found standing, and also to make other new cottages."[8]

Two days later, on July 25, White received his first good news since reaching the Outer Banks. The flyboat, with more colonists, had arrived from England. Captain Edward Spicer had never been to Virginia. Yet he had managed to sail the flyboat there all the way from England. The arrival of Captain Spicer and the rest of the colonists brought "great joy and comfort [to] the whole company," White declared.[9] Soon, all the English settlers were working side by side on Roanoke Island.

The Murder of George Howe

Just a few days after landing on Roanoke Island, George Howe, one of White's twelve assistants, wandered off alone. Howe wanted to catch crabs along the shore for food. Howe stripped down to his underclothes and found a forked stick to use as a crab-catching tool. Then, he waded into the shallow water. Suddenly, American Indians hidden in the shore reeds attacked him with their bows and arrows. Howe collapsed into the shallow water, his body struck sixteen times by arrows. To make sure that he was dead, the American Indians beat in his head with their wooden clubs. Then, they retreated in their canoes to the mainland.

The discovery of George Howe's murder shocked the other colonists. Two days later, on July 30, Captain Stafford sailed the pinnace southward, down the sound to Croatoan Island. With him sailed Manteo and twenty armed men. Manteo was not a Roanoke

Indian. He was a Croatoan. His mother was the leader of the friendly Croatoan tribe. During their visit to the Croatoan village, Stafford learned the story of what had happened to Grenville's fifteen men.

The Missing Fifteen

The Croatoan told the story of a day the previous autumn. Thirty American Indian warriors had hidden themselves among the trees near the English settlement. Two of the American Indians stepped from the woods. They approached two of Grenville's colonists with friendly gestures. The unsuspecting Englishmen allowed the American Indians to approach. Then, in an instant, one of the Indians drew his wooden war club. He smashed one of the Englishmen over the head with a deadly blow. With a yell, the hidden American Indians rushed from the woods and attacked. The surviving colonist ran into the settlement, shouting his alarm. Ten of the colonists took shelter in one of the cottages.

The Indians surged around the house and set fire to the thatch roof. The Englishmen choked on the smoke until they could stand it no longer. They charged out and battled with the Indians for more than an hour. During the fight, an arrow struck one colonist in the mouth and killed him. An American Indian also died when an Englishman picked up an arrow and stabbed him with it.

Dashing through the smoke and flames, nine colonists at last fled to the beach and their longboats.

Rowing hard, they retreated toward Hatarask Island. On the way, they picked up the last four colonists. The four had been away, collecting oysters from a stream. Altogether in the American Indian attack, two colonists had been killed. Others had been wounded. The thirteen survivors landed on a tiny island at the entrance of Hatarask harbor. They later left for an unknown destination.[10]

Grenville's colonists were never heard of again. According to the Croatoan, it was the Roanoke

John White drew this picture of an American Indian man and woman eating. They sit upon a mat with a wooden bowl of cooked meat between them.

Indians who had made the attacks on Grenville's men. It was also the Roanoke, they claimed, who had murdered George Howe.

Revenge at Dasemunkepeuc

After hearing this gruesome tale, Captain Stafford told the Croatoan to spread news among the region's American Indians. The English wanted peace. Stafford asked that the Roanoke chiefs be invited to gather at the Roanoke Island fort in seven days' time. The English would meet with them to discuss their problems. But a week passed and no Roanoke Indians came. It was then that Governor White and his assistants decided the Roanoke must be taught a lesson.

At midnight, on August 8, 1587, White sailed with Captain Stafford and twenty-three armed men in the pinnace to the mainland. Manteo went along as guide. The ship anchored near the Roanoke Indian village of Dasemunkepeuc. The Englishmen quietly circled through the woods. They placed themselves between the Indian longhouses and the sound. In that manner, they blocked any chance for the Roanoke to retreat. Through the trees they dimly saw a fire burning and around it some Indians sitting. The English attacked, shooting one of the Indians dead.[11]

The English hoped to get revenge against the Roanoke. But the attack was another terrible mistake. The American Indian they had killed was a Croatoan woman. In fact, all these American Indians were friendly Croatoans. One of them, recognizing Captain Stafford, ran forward calling out Stafford's name. The attack sputtered to a halt, as the English realized their awful error. These Croatoan had come from across the sound. They had landed at Dasemunkepeuc to gather up the corn and other crops abandoned by the Roanoke. The Roanoke themselves had fled the village long before. The entire attack was an unfortunate accident.

A Christening and a Baptism

Manteo had always been a good friend to the English. Perhaps Manteo smoothed over the tragedy at Dasemunkepeuc with the Croatoan. On August 13, 1587, the colonists showed their thankfulness. On that date, Governor White wrote in his journal, in the spelling of the times, "Our savage Manteo, by commandement of Sir Walter Raleigh, was christened in Roanoak, and called Lord thereof, and of Dasemongueponke, in reward of his faithfull service."[12] The English had persuaded Manteo to give up his Croatoan religion and become a Christian. In reward for his loyal service, they named Manteo chief of the Roanoke.

Five days later, on August 18, the English colonists smiled with special happiness. On that day, Eleanor White Dare gave birth to a daughter. The following Sunday, August 24, the baby was baptized. Her parents named her "Virginia." In rapid order, Manteo had been christened the first North American Indian

On August 24, 1587, the baby Virginia Dare was baptized on Roanoke Island. Virginia Dare was the first English child born in North America.

admitted to the Church of England, and Virginia Dare had become the first English child born in North America. The week after Virginia Dare was born, another pregnant colonist, Margery Harvie, also had a baby.

Governor White's Decision

All this time, Simon Ferdinando remained at anchor off the Outer Banks. His sailors were kept busy transferring supplies and equipment from the *Lion* and the

SOURCE DOCUMENT

[ELEANOR,] DAUGHTER TO THE GOVERNOR, AND WIFE TO ANANIAS DARE, ONE OF THE ASSISTANTS, WAS DELIVERED OF A DAUGHTER IN ROANOKE, AND THE SAME WAS CHRISTENED THERE THE SUNDAY FOLLOWING, AND BECAUSE THIS CHILD WAS THE FIRST CHRISTIAN BORN IN VIRGINIA, SHE WAS NAMED VIRGINIA.[13]

As governor, John White officially recorded the birth of his granddaughter on August 18, 1587.

flyboat to Roanoke Island. By August 21, the two ships were nearly ready to sail.

The colonists had decided that someone should return to England to obtain additional supplies. They looked upon Governor White as the best person for this important mission. On August 22, White explained in his journal, "the whole company, both of the Assistants and planters, came to the Governor and with one voice requested him to return, himself, into England, for the better and sooner obtaining of supplies . . ."[14]

At first, White refused their request. He felt responsible for bringing the colonists to Virginia. He also believed his knowledge of the region was needed to help make the colony a success. Roanoke Island was only a temporary base. White thought his advice would be needed when the time came to move to Chesapeake Bay. Also, he feared Sir Walter Raleigh would accuse him of deserting the colony. And it seems natural that he would be concerned about leaving his daughter and his baby granddaughter behind on Roanoke Island.

The next day, the colonists pleaded with White again. They insisted he could help the colony best by returning home to organize relief. They promised to take special care of his paints, brushes, and all the personal items that he would have to leave behind. In the end, their arguments finally persuaded the reluctant governor.

The Difficult Journey Home

White refused to sail on the *Lion* with Simon Ferdinando. Instead, on August 27, 1587, he hurriedly

---

SOURCE DOCUMENT

MAY IT PLEASE YOU, HER MAJESTY'S SUBJECTS OF ENGLAND, WE YOUR FRIENDS AND COUNTRYMEN, THE PLANTERS IN VIRGINIA, DO BY THESE PRESENTS LET YOU AND EVERY OF YOU TO UNDERSTAND THAT, FOR THE PRESENT AND SPEEDY SUPPLY OF CERTAIN OF OUR KNOWN AND APPARENT LACKS AND NEEDS, MOST . . . NECESSARY, FOR THE GOOD AND HAPPY PLANTING OF US OR ANY OTHER IN THIS LAND OF VIRGINIA, WE ALL, OF ONE MIND AND CONSENT, HAVE MOST EARNESTLY . . . REQUESTED JOHN WHITE, GOVERNOR OF THE PLANTERS IN VIRGINIA, TO PASS INTO ENGLAND. . . . [15]

Governor White had his assistants sign a document on August 25, 1587. The document proved he was returning to England at their special request.

boarded Captain Spicer's flyboat at Port Ferdinando. His voyage home had a very unhappy beginning. Twelve of the flyboat crewmen struggled to raise the anchor on its chain. The sailors crowded around the ship's capstan and began turning it. The capstan was like a giant screw. By turning the wooden spokes of the capstan, the anchor chain would wind up around it.

The sailors pushed the capstan spokes with all their strength. Suddenly, one of the capstan spokes broke, throwing the sailors off balance. Immediately the full weight of the anchor and chains yanked downward again toward the ocean bottom. The remaining capstan spokes spun around and around. They struck the sailors with terrific force. Ten of the ship's fifteen crewmen received broken ribs and other severe injuries. Unable to raise the anchor, Captain Spicer finally ordered the chain cut so the ship could set sail.

With most of its crew injured, the flyboat still managed to sail along behind the *Lion* for three weeks. At last, the two ships neared the Azore Islands. Then, a fierce storm rose and blew for six days straight. The roaring waves tossed the flyboat about like a toy. White and all the crew feared they would surely drown. Two of the injured sailors died during this time. Unable to land in the Azores, the flyboat ran out of drinking water. The sailors drank whatever they could find onboard: beer, wine, and foul-tasting water.[16]

Fifty days after leaving the Outer Banks, a lookout aboard the flyboat finally spotted land. The battered ship reached Ireland on October 16, 1587. It was too late to save some of the crewmen. Within four days of reaching land, four more of the injured sailors died. Eager to report to Sir Walter Raleigh, John White left the flyboat behind. Boarding another ship, White hurried on to England.

8

JOHN WHITE'S ADVENTURES

John White arrived in Southampton, England, on November 8, 1587. As he walked along the streets, he realized much had changed since the day he had left. Now it seemed England was in real danger of being conquered by its enemy, Spain. In Spain, King Philip II was preparing a huge fleet of warships, the Spanish Armada. In English ports, navy ships were being gathered to defend England from the expected invasion.

The Defense of England

Governor White soon met with Sir Walter Raleigh. White urgently made his request for supplies for his colonists. In the middle of a full-scale war, however, the needs of a small colony in Virginia did not seem very important. Still, Raleigh agreed to try to help. He asked Sir Richard Grenville to organize a supply fleet at Bideford, England. At the same time, White searched for more colonists.

By March 31, 1588, Grenville's new fleet of eight ships was loaded and ready to set sail for Virginia. But at the very last moment royal orders arrived. They instructed Grenville to add his ships to the naval fleet being assembled at Plymouth. Grenville's ships and sailors were required to help defend England in its national emergency.

Deeply disappointed, White begged for permission to keep two of Grenville's smaller ships. At least then a few new colonists and some supplies would get to Roanoke. White finally received permission to take the 30-ton *Brave* and the 25-ton *Roe*. They both sailed on April 22, 1588, with fifteen new colonists and a small cargo of supplies.

Captain Arthur Facy commanded this expedition. Unfortunately, John White soon discovered that Captain Facy and his sailors were not interested in a long voyage to Virginia. Much like Simon Ferdinando and his sailors, they were more interested in capturing ships for the prize money. Facy and his sailors did not care if the ships they captured belonged to Spain or to other countries. On their very first day at sea, the *Brave* and the *Roe* attacked two ships they chanced upon. One was from Scotland, and the other was from France. "These we boarded also," White reported in his journal, "and took from them whatsoever we could find worth the taking."[1]

The Tables Are Turned

For nearly two weeks, the *Brave* and the *Roe* chased after every ship they saw. The *Brave*, with John White aboard, soon lost sight of the *Roe*. Still, Captain Facy refused to set a course for Virginia. Then, on May 6, Facy learned the danger of being a privateer aboard a little ship. Off the Madeira Islands, a large French warship attacked the *Brave*. Cannonballs ripped through the *Brave*'s sails and rigging. The heavy iron balls smashed into the wooden hull. In the violent sea battle, French sailors climbed aboard the *Brave*. They fought the English sailors in hand-to-hand combat. It was a bloody battle. Dozens of men were killed and wounded. John White found himself in the thick of the fight. "I myself was wounded twice in the head," he later wrote, "once with a sword and another time with a pike, and hurt also in the side of the buttock with a shot."[2] A pike was a weapon shaped like a long, heavy spear.

When the smoke cleared, the English had lost the battle. Facy was forced to surrender. John White and the surviving English passengers and crew grimly watched. The French sailors transferred the *Brave*'s cargo onto their own ship. All the supplies intended for the colony were taken. White reported, "We were [forced] to break off our voyage . . . and the same night to set our course for England."[3]

On May 22, the beaten English crew docked the *Brave* at Bideford. A few weeks later, White learned that the *Roe* also had returned to England. In his journal, he sadly noted that both ships had returned "without performing our intended voyage for the relief of the planters in Virginia."[4]

The Spanish Armada

The English anxiously expected the attack of the Spanish Armada every day throughout the spring and summer of 1588. In July, the great enemy fleet was finally sighted entering the English Channel. One hundred thirty great Spanish ships filled the channel. It was a spectacular display of power. Many of the large ships were of the type called galleons. Eight thousand sailors and nineteen thousand soldiers covered the decks of these Spanish ships.

English naval leaders Sir John Hawkins and Sir Francis Drake had done their best to prepare for the fight. The English fleet included two hundred ships of various sizes. They were manned by about sixteen thousand sailors. Many of the English ships were smaller and faster than the giant Spanish galleons. They were also easier to steer. Many were equipped with long-range cannons. At a distance, the English cannonballs would be able to strike the Spanish galleons without being in danger of return fire.

The Spanish Armada anchored in the French harbor of Calais on July 27. The next night, the English made a surprise attack. English sailors set some of their own ships on fire on purpose. They bravely steered them in among the anchored Spanish ships. They hoped to set the Armada ablaze. Many Spanish sailors panicked. They cut their ship's anchor cables and fled the harbor, sailing in all directions. The fight continued throughout the night and into the next day. The English captains struck repeatedly, sinking enemy ships

The great Spanish Armada is shown here sailing into the English Channel in July 1588. England's hastily assembled navy sailed out to battle the dreaded Spanish invasion fleet. The future of England depended on the outcome.

with cannonballs. In the days that followed, escaping Spanish ships sailed directly into a violent storm. Many ships were wrecked on the rocky coasts of Scotland and Ireland. Fewer than eighty ships finally reached the safety of Spain. The mighty Spanish Armada had been beaten. Throughout England, people cheered their navy's amazing victory.

John White's Mission

All the while, John White yearned to send help to the colonists on Roanoke Island. Still nursing his wounds, he pleaded again with Sir Walter Raleigh in London. Queen Elizabeth had given Raleigh large estates in Ireland. Ireland was a country that England was trying to conquer and control. Raleigh's attention was required to protect his Irish lands and make them show a profit. Just then, he did not have the time or money to equip any ships for White himself. So Raleigh arranged for a business partner, merchant William Sanderson, to find a ship for White.

Early in 1590, Sanderson prepared the 80-ton *Moonlight* to sail to Virginia with supplies. In command was White's old friend Captain Edward Spicer. For safety, Raleigh arranged that the *Moonlight* would sail to North America with an English privateering expedition. The expedition was being organized by a merchant named John Watts. Watts's largest ship was the 150-ton *Hopewell*, commanded by Captain Abraham Cocke. He owned two smaller ships, as well, the *Little John*, and the *John Evangelist*.

In February 1590, White brought several new colonists to the docks on the Thames River. It was where Watts's ships were being readied. When it came time to board the *Hopewell*, however, John Watts and Captain Cocke refused to let them up the boarding plank. "I was by the owner and Commanders of the ships," recalled White, "denied to have any passengers, or any thing else transported in any of the said ships, saving only myself and my chest. . . . "[5] Watts was sending his three ships out privateering. He did not want a lot of colonists crowding the decks and getting in the way.

Aboard the *Hopewell*

On March 20, the *Hopewell*, the *Little John*, and the *John Evangelist* set sail from Plymouth, England. Aboard the *Hopewell*, John White eagerly looked forward to seeing his family in Virginia again. The supply ship, the *Moonlight*, was not yet ready. But White hoped it would follow close behind.

Near the Canary Islands, Captain Cocke's privateers captured a ship loaded with wine and cinnamon. The captured ship was sent back to England. The *Hopewell*, the *Little John*, and the *John Evangelist* continued onward. They swiftly crossed the Atlantic Ocean in twenty-three days. When they reached the Caribbean Sea, the *Hopewell* and the *John Evangelist* captured the Spanish ship *Trinidad* near Puerto Rico. It was loaded with a cargo of leather hides and ginger. The roving sailors next landed on the small island of Mona, where they burned a Spanish village and captured a pinnace. The English then cruised along the coast of Hispañiola. If the *Moonlight* was on its way, it had been agreed it would meet with them there.

On July 2, Captain Spicer finally arrived at the meeting place with the *Moonlight*. A second ship, *Conclude,* a pinnace, had also crossed the ocean in company with the *Moonlight*. For the moment then, Captain Cocke's English fleet consisted of seven vessels. They were the *Hopewell*, the *Little John*, the *John*

Evangelist, the *Moonlight*, and the *Conclude*, as well as two captured ships. That very afternoon, sharp-eyed lookouts sighted a fleet of Spanish treasure ships. The English ships chased after them into the darkness of night. By dawn the following morning, the English ships were widely scattered. Only the *Moonlight* and the *Hopewell* remained in sight of each other. Together they pursued a large Spanish ship. Minute by minute, they gained on the Spanish ship, until at last they were within cannon range.

The English ships fired their cannons. Cannonballs struck the Spanish ship, smashing into the wooden hull and tearing through the canvas sails. The attack lasted for several hours. Finally, the battered Spanish ship, *El Buen Jesus*, surrendered. The ship was a fine prize. Its valuable cargo included one hundred tons of ginger, six thousand hides of leather, two hundred boxes of sugar, as well as chests of pepper and other spices. Captain Cocke put English sailors aboard and ordered them to sail the prize ship back to England.

Signal Fires

Not until July 28 did Captain Cocke agree to steer northward for Virginia. Unfortunately, the English ships sailed directly into a hurricane off the coast of Florida. For five days and nights, heavy rain and roaring seas roughly pitched the ships about. The weather-beaten ships reached Hatarask Island on the Outer Banks on August 15, 1590. They then cruised up the coast to Port Ferdinando.

At last, Roanoke Island was just a few miles away across Pamlico Sound. Gazing in that direction, the sailors spied a great cloud of smoke hanging in the sky. They thought it might be a signal fire lit by the colonists at Roanoke.

The English ships spent the night anchored at Port Ferdinando. Shortly after dawn on August 16, sailors lowered two longboats into the water. Taking up the oars, they began rowing for the gap leading into Pamlico Sound. Captain Cocke commanded one of the boats. Captain Spicer was in charge of the other. John White was seated among Captain Cocke's oarsmen.

Halfway to the inlet, Governor White noticed "another great smoke" to the south on Hatarask Island.[6] It seemed to rise from a large Outer Banks sand hill the English called Kenricks Mount. White, Cocke, and Spicer thought it might be another signal fire. It might have been started by colonists standing watch at Kenricks Mount. The governor and the two captains changed their plans. As White later explained, "[We] thought good to go to that second smoke first."[7]

White and the English sailors landed on Hatarask Island and began hiking southward over the sand. After several miles, they realized the smoke was farther away than they thought. It was a very long hike all the way to Kenricks Mount. They discovered that the smoke was caused by fields of burning grass. It was a very hot, dry summer. Perhaps the intense heat of the sun had set the grass on fire.

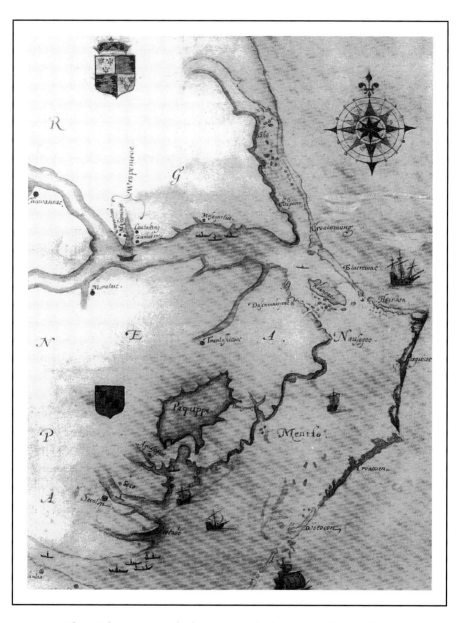

John White painted this map of the part of the North American coast which the English explored in the 1580s. Between the Outer Banks and the mainland, Roanoke Island (spelled Roanoac) can be seen to the left of the ship drawn halfway up the picture.

On sore feet, the tired men walked back to the longboats. The boats were beached on the ocean side of the inlet. The entire day had been wasted. They had searched Hatarask for colonists and a signal fire that were not there. The men decided to wait until the next day to continue their trip to Roanoke Island.

Death at Port Ferdinando

Throughout the night, the wind increased and the ocean waves rose higher and higher. By morning, it seemed certain a storm was coming to the Outer Banks. John White, Captain Cocke, Captain Spicer, and the longboat crewmen set out again for Roanoke Island. They would have to pass through the Port Ferdinando inlet in order to enter Pamlico Sound.

Captain Cocke's longboat was rowed in first. The sailors pulled hard at their oars. On this day, the water seemed especially rough. Suddenly, a huge wave flooded the longboat. White joined the frantic sailors in bailing water out of the boat. For a time, it appeared the boat would sink. With hard rowing and careful steering, the sailors finally managed to pass through the gap. They beached the boat on the inside of the sound.

Next it was Captain Spicer's turn to guide the second longboat through the difficult inlet. From the beach, White fearfully watched as Spicer's boat entered the narrow passage. The boat was halfway through when a great wave struck. It tipped the boat completely over. White helplessly stared as the awful scene unfolded before him. "The men stayed with the boat," he declared, "some in it, others clinging to it. But . . . some of the men were forced to let go their hold and try to wade ashore. The sea beat them down again and again. "[8]

The heaving waves turned the flooded boat over again. White saw Captain Spicer and sailor Ralph Skinner trying to hold on. But at last they lost their grips. The waves dragged them under the salty water. White never saw them again. The rest of the long-boat's sailors also struggled to stay alive. "Four of the men . . . " exclaimed White, "were saved by Captain Cocke. As soon as he saw their boat capsize, [Cocke] took off his clothes and, with four others . . . rowed out as fast as possible and saved four of them."[9]

Sadly, it was too late to save the rest. Of the eleven sailors who had been aboard the longboat, a total of seven drowned: Thomas Bevins, Robert Coleman, Edward Kelborne, Edward Kelly, Ralph Skinner, Edward Spicer, and a surgeon named Hance.[10] Their bodies were washed out to sea.

The Carved Message

The drowning of Captain Spicer and his sailors in the inlet had been a terrible thing. But White remained anxious to continue across the sound to Roanoke Island. The dazed sailors around him, however, had other ideas. "They were all of one mind not to go any further to seek the planters," described White.[11] They wanted only to return to the safety of their ships. They pointed to the darkening clouds overhead. They insisted that a storm would soon bring even rougher seas. White was grateful when Captain Cocke finally decided they would continue to Roanoke. Inspired by their leaders, the other sailors agreed to continue.[12]

The sailors managed to pull Captain Spicer's boat to shore. Now both boats were boarded again. The Englishmen began rowing across Pamlico Sound. Ahead, White watched the smoke that still rose above Roanoke Island. He hoped that, unlike the smoke at Kenricks Mount, this was the smoke of a true signal fire.

The two longboats reached the island after dark. It was too late to land safely, so the men waited on the boats overnight. They played English songs upon a trumpet and called out. But they heard only silence in return. The next morning, August 18, 1590, the men landed.

Curiously, it had been exactly three years since White's granddaughter Virginia Dare had been born. Surely, White must have been eager to see her again. He must have felt disappointed when the landing party soon discovered that the smoke was from another natural fire. Perhaps it had been started by lightning, or perhaps by the heat of the sun.

The Englishmen hiked along the shore toward the settlement. On the way, they found a tree with the letters "CRO" carved upon it. At the settlement, the men discovered another carving. Cut into the trunk of another tree was the word "CROATOAN." To the sailors, the carvings were a complete mystery. But John White thought he understood their meanings.

When he left Roanoke in 1587, the colonists had promised to carve a message if they moved to Chesapeake or elsewhere. White believed the word CROATOAN meant that at least some of the colonists had gone to Croatoan Island. White told the sailors he and the colonists had also agreed to something else. If the colonists were in trouble, they had promised to add a cross to their carved message. But no cross was carved on the trees with CRO or CROATOAN. White hoped his family and friends were safe. He guessed the colony had abandoned Roanoke Island and had gone thirty miles southward to live among the friendly Croatoan Indians.

The Dug-Up Chests

The Englishmen continued to look for more clues of the missing colonists. White recalled that he and Captain Cocke "went along by the water side towards the point of the creek [northeast of the fort] to see if we could find any of their boats or pinnace, but we could perceive no sign of them . . ."[13]

White and Cocke walked back to the fort. There they were met by several sailors who had made a discovery. They had found five chests that had been buried. White and Cocke were led to the place. The chests had been broken open. Their contents were scattered over the ground. White saw that " . . . my books were torn from the covers, the frames of my pictures

Many of John White's drawings were lost at sea or destroyed by weather after the chests they were in were broken open. This engraving by Theodor de Bry is from one of White's drawings that survived. It shows the method that American Indians of the Roanoke area used to make canoes.

and maps were rotted and broken by rain, and my armor was almost eaten through with rust."[14] White guessed Roanoke Indians from Dasemunkepeuc had secretly watched the colonists leave the island. When they were gone, the Indians had entered the abandoned settlement in search of useful items left behind. Surely, the Indians were the ones who had dug up these buried chests.[15]

White tried not to think of his destroyed possessions. Instead, he gave all his thoughts to the carved messages. They gave him hope that the colonists were still alive. "Although it much grieved me to see such spoil of my goods," he later declared, "yet on the other side I greatly joyed that I had safely found a certain token of their safe being at Croatoan."[16]

Lost Anchors

All that remained was for John White to sail to Croatoan. There he expected to find his missing colonists. But with each passing hour, the sky turned darker and it became windier. Captain Cocke's sailors grumbled that a mighty storm was fast approaching.

The longboats returned over the choppy water to the anchored ships at Port Ferdinando. After everyone got on board the ships, the sea got even rougher. It was then that someone remembered that six men had been left on the Outer Banks nearby. They had been sent to shore to fill casks with fresh water. Captain Cocke ordered a longboat lowered. Five brave men rowed back to shore to pick them up.

They brought their comrades back through the dangerous sea, but they had to leave the water casks behind.

That night, the *Hopewell* and the *Moonlight* pitched and rolled on the ocean waves off Port Ferdinando. At dawn, White and Cocke decided to try to sail to Croatoan.[17] But the weather was very bad now. As the sailors raised the *Hopewell*'s anchor, the chain broke. The ship began to drift helplessly toward shore. It was in danger of being tossed by the great waves into shallow water and wrecked. The sailors quickly dropped a second anchor. But it was also lost. Only one anchor was left. Captain Cocke shouted orders. His sailors strained at the steering wheel. They hauled at the canvas sails. Slowly, the ship inched out of danger and into safer, deeper water further out to sea. But it was clear that the *Hopewell* was unsafe remaining near the Outer Banks. The pounding waves had grown too dangerous.

Sailors crowded around Captain Cocke. They begged him to sail directly to England. White and Captain Cocke discussed the situation. They offered the unhappy crewmen a different plan. The ships would sail south all the way to the Caribbean Sea. In the Caribbean, they could collect fresh water and food. Perhaps they could even capture a Spanish treasure ship or two. In the spring, when the weather calmed, they would return to visit Croatoan. John Bedford, captain of the *Moonlight*, rejected this plan. He claimed that his ship was too battered and leaky to make the long voyage south. Captain Cocke allowed the *Moonlight* to set sail that night for England. The sailors of the *Hopewell*, however, were persuaded to sail south.

Ruined Plans

Captain Cocke selected the Caribbean island of Trinidad as the proper place for the *Hopewell* to spend the winter. The *Hopewell* set its course for Trinidad. The stormy weather, however, soon overtook the little ship. The driving rain and violent winds pushed the *Hopewell* far out into the open ocean. By the time the storm finally passed, the ship was many miles off course. It was closer to the Azore Islands than any other land. Captain Cocke decided to head for the Azores.

The *Hopewell* reached the Azore Islands on September 17. The ship was now halfway home to England. It did not make sense to go to Trinidad now. Captain Cocke decided to steer for England instead. It seems, by then, John White was too exhausted to argue. In his journal, White simply noted in October 1590, "Saturday the 24. We came in safety, God be thanked, to an anchor at Plymouth."[18]

Governor John White's three-year effort had failed. He had not reached his colonists and his family in Virginia. His settlers may have been safe and happy at Croatoan. But the 117 English men, women, and children abandoned on the vast North American continent in 1587 were never heard from again. They have come to be known in history as "The Lost Colony of Roanoke." In time, John White settled in Newtown, County Cork, Ireland. It is thought he spent his last years there.[19] It is unknown if he ever made another attempt to return to North America to find his missing daughter and granddaughter.

The search for the missing Roanoke Island colonists has gone on for the past four hundred years. Some scholars believe that the colonists did indeed abandon Roanoke Island to live with the friendly Croatoan Indians. Some guess disease or perhaps starvation killed them all. Others think that they tried to sail back to England in their small pinnace only to sink and drown in the vast Atlantic Ocean.

SOLVING A MYSTERY

Sir Walter Raleigh's Interest in America

In 1590, the six years given to Sir Walter Raleigh in his royal charter came to an end. He lost his exclusive right to explore North America. He also soon fell out of favor with Queen Elizabeth.

In 1592, Raleigh secretly married Elizabeth Throckmorton, one of Queen Elizabeth's ladies-in-waiting. Ladies-in-waiting were women who served many duties as the queen's personal servants. When she learned of the marriage, the English queen fell into a jealous rage. It seemed she wanted Raleigh all for herself. She did not like the fact that he had given his love to another. For a time, she imprisoned Raleigh and his wife in the Tower of London. When they were released at last, she allowed them to retire to Ireland.

In 1595, Raleigh finally sailed the Atlantic Ocean himself. But he did not voyage to Virginia and Roanoke Island. Instead, he landed and searched for gold in South America. He explored an area called Guiana, at the mouth of the Orinoco River in present-day Venezuela. But Raleigh returned to England without finding gold. In 1602, Raleigh finally sent a man named Samuel Mace to search for the Virginia colonists. Mace landed far to the south of Croatoan near Cape Fear on the Outer Banks. There he traded with the American Indians for a month and then returned to England. Mace brought no news of the lost colony.

A Date with the Executioner

In 1603, Queen Elizabeth died at the age of sixty-nine. She had no child to take over her kingdom. As a result, England's noblemen chose King James I of Scotland to sit upon the English throne. In 1604, King James signed a peace treaty with Spain. Unlike Queen Elizabeth, King James never considered Sir Walter Raleigh one of his favorites. In fact, King James became convinced that Raleigh was plotting against him. He charged Raleigh with treason and threw him into the Tower of London again. A trial found Raleigh guilty of treason, and he was sentenced to death.

Raleigh spent years sitting in his cell with death awaiting him. Finally, however, he persuaded King

James to give him another chance to find the fabled gold of Guiana. By 1616, King James and the royal treasury were deep in debt. Raleigh was in his middle sixties when he was released from prison to make his second voyage to Guiana. The trip proved a total failure. Many of Raleigh's adventurers died of sickness in the South American jungle.

Raleigh returned to England from his failed expedition. Soon after, his death sentence was finally carried out. On October 29, 1618, Raleigh climbed the steps of the scaffold at the Tower of London. He was to be beheaded. Raleigh was witty, even in the face of certain death. He asked to see the executioner's axe. When the executioner showed it to him, Raleigh joked, "This is a sharp medicine, but it is a sure cure for all diseases."[1]

The Search for Roanoke Survivors

Although the Roanoke colonists could not be found, they were not forgotten in England. In September 1605, London actors performed a play entitled *Eastward Ho*. The comedy was written by Ben Jonson, George Chapman, and John Marston. In the play, a character named Captain Seagull described one of the wonders of far away Virginia. "A Whole Country of English is there," Captain Seagull exclaims, "bred of those that were left there in ['87.] They have married with the Indians and make them bring forth as beautiful faces as any we have in England."[2]

On April 26, 1607, Captain Christopher Newport sailed into Chesapeake Bay with 144 English settlers aboard a small fleet of ships. They founded a new colony called Jamestown on the James River in present-day Virginia. One of the goals of these colonists was to search for survivors of the Roanoke settlement. While the Jamestown fort was being built, Captain Newport sent a longboat to explore upriver. The exploring party journeyed some eighty miles into the wilderness. At a bend in the river, they were startled to make a strange discovery in an American Indian village. Jamestown colonist George Percy described that he saw "a savage boy, about the age of ten years, which had a head of hair of a perfect yellow and a reasonable white skin, which is a miracle amongst all the savages."[3] Some historians wonder if this boy was the result of the marriage of an American Indian and a Roanoke colonist.

The Jamestown colonists made repeated efforts to find the Roanoke colonists. While in command at Jamestown, Captain John Smith sent two search parties to the south, looking for evidence of them. But they found no trace. Many historians think that the carvings John White found at Roanoke mean that the colonists did indeed take refuge on Croatoan Island. Unfortunately, no English ever visited Croatoan to search for them.

Some scholars believe that many of the Roanoke colonists journeyed north to Chesapeake Bay. There they began life among the Chesapeake Indians. The great chief fighting for control of that region was Powhatan, the father of Pocahontas. In 1607, just

English colonists landed in Chesapeake Bay on April 26, 1607. They immediately went to work building a new Virginia settlement called Jamestown. It would prove to be the first lasting English colony in North America.

before Jamestown was founded, it is believed that Powhatan attacked some enemy Chesapeake tribes. It is thought that Powhatan killed many Chesapeakes and the English colonists who lived with them. Englishman Samuel Purchas published a book in 1625. It included stories told by Captain Smith. "Powhatan confessed that he had been at the murder of that colony," Purchas wrote, "and showed to Captain Smith a musket barrel and a bronze [cannon] and certain pieces of iron which had been theirs."[4]

A portrait of Captain John Smith. While in command at Jamestown, Captain Smith unsuccessfully tried to find the missing Roanoke colonists. American Indian chief Powhatan later told Smith he had seen the Roanoke settlers killed during an Indian war in 1607.

The Passage of Time

In time, the English expanded their claims to North America. Settlers occupied Roanoke Island again in 1670. The island became part of England's North Carolina Colony. When Americans claimed their independence from England in 1776, Roanoke Island became part of the United States.

On the morning of April 7, 1819, the steamboat *Albemarle* docked at Roanoke Island. United States President James Monroe stepped ashore to visit the historic island. A local newspaper, the *Edenton Gazette*, described the president's tour. President Monroe and his party had come "to view the remains of the Fort," the story reported, "the traces of which are still distinctly visible, which is said to have been erected by the first colony of Sir Walter Raleigh."[5]

For years, historians have tried to determine exactly where the colony was located on the island. In 1947 and 1948, archaeologist J. C. Harrington carefully shoveled away dirt. He dug where he believed Colonel Ralph Lane's original fort could be found. Harrington discovered the remains of a diamond-shaped, earthwork fort on the northern tip of Roanoke Island. Today a reconstructed fort, about 50 square feet in size, can be visited at the Fort Raleigh National Historic Site. But Harrington failed to discover evidence of a settlement nearby. It is possible, after all, that the colonists built more than one fort. Centuries of winds and tides have greatly changed Roanoke Island. The length of the island today is about four

President James Monroe visited the Roanoke site more than two hundred years after the colony disappeared.

miles shorter than it was in 1590. Erosion has eaten away at least a quarter of a mile of land at the north end of the island. Still, some historians believe archaeologists might find the Roanoke settlement at Baum Point if they dug there.

New Research

In 1998, new scientific research yielded information on what might have happened at Roanoke. Scientists studied the annual growth rings of ancient cypress trees growing in the region. By cutting cross sections from the tree trunks, the growth rings can be counted year by year. Each ring reveals by its thickness how much moisture was in the soil in any given year.

The scientists discovered that the Roanoke colonists arrived in North Carolina at a bad time. It was during the worst drought in eight hundred years. It was hot, dry, and rainless. The Lost Colony "might well have survived if not for the drought," declared Dr. Warren Billings, a historian at the University of New Orleans.[6] Archaeologist Dennis Blanton remarked, "If the English had tried to find a worse time to launch their settlements in the New World, they could not have done so."[7]

In such a terrible drought, lack of rain would have killed the corn crops. Perhaps the colonists starved as a result. Perhaps they fought the American Indians for what little food remained. Maybe they tried to escape Roanoke and died in the attempt. Scientists, archaeologists, and historians will continue to search for answers. But it is possible that we will never know what definitely happened to the Lost Colony.

Many people regard Sir Walter Raleigh's efforts to establish a colony at Roanoke as a failure. But others point out its success. The little settlement at Roanoke marked England's first real effort to colonize North America. Other determined English started other colonies: at Jamestown, Virginia; Plymouth, Massachusetts, and all along the Atlantic coast. The colonies these English established would be more permanent. The seeds of hope first planted at Roanoke would grow into thirteen thriving American colonies. Some might even argue that the history of the United States began four hundred years ago with Sir Walter Raleigh's experiment at Roanoke Island.

★ TIMELINE ★

1000—Norseman Leif Eriksson establishes a settlement called Vinland for about a year somewhere along the coast of present-day Canada.

1492—Christopher Columbus, sailing for Spain, discovers the New World on October 12.

1497—John Cabot makes first successful exploration of North America in English ships; Cabot lands at Newfoundland.

1519—Spanish soldier Hernán Cortes conquers the Aztec Empire of present-day Mexico.

1538—Spaniard Francisco Pizarro finishes his conquest of the Incan Empire on the western coast of South America.

1578—Sir Humphrey Gilbert receives a charter from England's Queen Elizabeth I to explore North America.

1583—Gilbert lands in Newfoundland and formally claims the region for England; He dies at sea before returning to England.

1584—Walter Raleigh receives an exploration charter from Queen Elizabeth; Raleigh sends captains Philip Amadas and Arthur Barlowe to search for a place to establish an English colony; Amadas and Barlowe discover the Outer Banks of present-day North Carolina; They make contact with the Algonquian Indians, and Captain Barlowe visits Roanoke Island.

1585—England goes to war against Spain; Raleigh sends Sir Richard Grenville to the Outer Banks to establish an English colony; In July, Grenville explores Pamlico Sound and visits American Indian villages; In August, Roanoke Island is chosen as the English settlement site; In September, when Grenville returns to England, Lieutenant Colonel Ralph Lane is left in charge of the colony; Lane sends out exploring parties during the winter.

1586—Roanoke chief Wingina is beheaded by the English; In June, Sir Francis Drake brings a fleet to the Outer Banks; After a hurricane, Ralph Lane returns to England with his colonists aboard Drake's ships; Two weeks later, Grenville returns to the Outer Banks with supply ships; Grenville leaves fifteen men on Roanoke Island.

1587—In May, Governor John White leaves England with 117 settlers on a voyage for Chesapeake Bay; In July, the colonists are forced to settle on Roanoke Island; On August 18, Virginia Dare becomes the first English child born in North America; Soon after, White returns to England to obtain supplies.

1588—In May, White fails in his attempt to return to Virginia aboard the *Brave*; In July and August, English warships beats the Spanish Armada in a great sea battle in the English Channel.

1590—In August, White returns to Virginia aboard the *Hopewell*; He finds the Roanoke settlement abandoned and the word CROATOAN carved on a tree post; The *Hopewell* is forced by bad weather to return to England before it can visit Croatoan Island.

1595—Sir Walter Raleigh explores Guiana on the coast of present-day Venezuela.

1607—In April, the English establish a permanent settlement at Jamestown, Virginia.

1616—Sir Walter Raleigh returns to Guiana in another failed attempt to find gold.

1618—Raleigh is beheaded for treason on October 29.

1947–1948—An archaeologist, J. C. Harrington, excavates a fort on Roanoke Island; It is now part of the Fort Raleigh National Historical Site.

1998—Scientists analyze tree growth rings and discover the worst drought in eight hundred years occurred just when the English attempted to settle at Roanoke in 1587.

★ CHAPTER NOTES ★

Chapter 1. Croatoan

1. Stefan Lorant, *The New World* (New York: Duell, Sloan and Pearce, 1965), p. 175.

2. Ibid.

3. David N. Durant, *Ralegh's Lost Colony* (New York: Atheneum, 1981), p. 147.

4. David Beers Quinn, *Set Fair For Roanoke* (Chapel Hill: University of North Carolina Press, 1985), p. 326.

5. Lorant, pp. 175–176.

6. Ibid.

Chapter 2. The New World

1. Cecil Jane, trans., *The Journal of Christopher Columbus* (New York: Bonanza Books, 1989), p. 191.

2. David Stick, *Roanoke Island: The Beginnings of English America* (Chapel Hill: University of North Carolina Press, 1983), p. 29.

3. David N. Durant, *Ralegh's Lost Colony* (New York: Atheneum, 1981), p. 8.

Chapter 3. Amadas and Barlowe Set Sail

1. Stefan Lorant, *The New World* (New York: Duell, Sloan and Pearce, 1965), p. 125.

2. Ibid., p. 126.

3. Ibid.

4. Ibid.

5. Ibid.

6. Ibid., p. 129.

7. David Stick, *Roanoke Island: The Beginnings of English America* (Chapel Hill: University of North Carolina Press, 1983), pp. 39–42.

8. Lorant, p. 127.

9. Ibid.

10. Ibid., p. 128.

11. Stick, p. 116.

12. Lorant, p. 130.

13. Ibid.

14. Karen Ordahl Kupperman, *Roanoke: The Abandoned Colony* (Savage, Maryland: Rowman & Allanheld Publishers, Inc., 1984), p. 72.

15. Lorant, p. 131.

16. Ibid.

17. Ibid.

18. Stick, p. 49.

19. David N. Durant, *Ralegh's Lost Colony* (New York: Atheneum, 1981), p. 20.

Chapter 4. Sir Richard Grenville's Expedition

1. Lee Miller, *Roanoke* (New York: Arcade Publishing, 2000), p. 88.

2. David N. Durant, *Ralegh's Lost Colony* (New York: Atheneum, 1981), pp. 49–50.

3. David Beers Quinn, *Set Fair For Roanoke* (Chapel Hill: University of North Carolina Press, 1985), pp. 77–80.

Chapter 5. Ralph Lane in Command

1. Stefan Lorant, *The New World* (New York: Duell, Sloan and Pearce, 1960), p. 246.

2. Ibid.

3. Karen Ordahl Kupperman, *Roanoke: The Abandoned Colony* (Savage, Maryland: Rowman & Allanheld Publishers, Inc., 1984), p. 48.

4. David Beers Quinn, *Set Fair For Roanoke* (Chapel Hill: University of North Carolina Press, 1985), p. 105.

5. Ibid., p. 89.

6. Ibid., p. 104.

7. Lee Miller, *Roanoke* (New York: Arcade Publishing, 2000), p. 102.

8. Ibid., p. 103.

9. David Stick, *Roanoke Island: The Beginnings of English America* (Chapel Hill: University of North Carolina Press, 1983), p. 126.

10. Ibid.

11. Quinn, p. 123.

12. Karen Ordahl Kupperman, "Roanoke Lost," *American Heritage*, August 1985, p. 86.

Chapter 6. Sir Francis Drake

1. David Stick, *Roanoke Island: The Beginnings of English America* (Chapel Hill: University of North Carolina Press, 1983), p. 145.

2. Ibid.

3. Ibid., pp. 148–149.

4. David Beers Quinn, *Set Fair For Roanoke* (Chapel Hill: University of North Carolina Press, 1985), p. 146.

Chapter 7. Return to Roanoke

1. David N. Durant, *Ralegh's Lost Colony* (New York: Atheneum, 1981), p. 103.

2. Ivor Noel Hume, *The Virginia Adventure* (New York: Alfred A. Knopf, 1994), p. 57.

3. Stefan Lorant, *The New World* (New York: Duell, Sloan and Pearce, 1960), p. 155.

4. Karen Ordahl Kupperman, *Roanoke: The Abandoned Colony* (Savage, Maryland: Rowman and Allanheld Publishers, Inc., 1984), p. 111.

5. Ibid., p. 113.

6. Lorant, p. 158.

7. David Beers Quinn, *Set Fair For Roanoke* (Chapel Hill: University of North Carolina Press, 1985), p. 280.

8. Durant, pp. 115–116.

9. Quinn, p. 282.

10. Lorant, p. 160.

11. Ibid., p. 161.

12. Durant, p. 120.

13. Lee Miller, *Roanoke* (New York: Arcade Publishing, 2000), p. 74.

14. Quinn, p. 289.

15. Ibid., p. 291.

16. Lorant, p. 164.

Chapter 8. John White's Adventures

1. David Stick, *Roanoke Island: The Beginnings of English America* (Chapel Hill: University of North Carolina Press, 1983), p. 191.

2. David Beers Quinn, *Set Fair For Roanoke* (Chapel Hill: University of North Carolina Press, 1985), p. 305.

3. Stick, p. 193.

4. Ibid.

5. Ivor Noel Hume, *The Virginia Adventure* (New York: Alfred A. Knopf, 1994), p. 69.

6. Stick, pp. 205–206.

7. Ibid.

8. Stefan Lorant, *The New World* (New York: Duell, Sloan and Pearce, 1960), pp. 174–175.

9. Ibid.

10. Ibid.

11. Stick, p. 208.

12. Lorant, p. 175.

13. Quinn, p. 329.

14. Lorant, p. 176.

15. David N. Durant, *Ralegh's Lost Colony* (New York: Atheneum, 1981), pp. 149–150.

16. Lee Miller, *Roanoke* (New York: Arcade Publishing, 2000), p. 15.

17. Lorant, p. 176.

18. Miller, p. 18.

19. Durant, p. 152.

Chapter 9. Solving a Mystery

1. Karen Ordahl Kupperman, *Roanoke: The Abandoned Colony* (Savage, Maryland: Rowman and Allanheld Publishers, Inc., 1984), p. 157.

2. David N. Durant, *Ralegh's Lost Colony* (New York: Atheneum, 1981), p. 158.

3. Lee Miller, *Roanoke* (New York: Arcade Publishing, 2000), p. 212.

4. David Beers Quinn, *Set Fair For Roanoke* (Chapel Hill: University of North Carolina Press, 1985), p. 365.

5. David Stick, *Roanoke Island: The Beginnings of English America* (Chapel Hill: University of North Carolina Press, 1983), p. 228.

6. William K. Stevens, "Drought May Have Doomed Lost Colony," *The New York Times*, April 24, 1998, pp. A1–A14.

7. Katurah Mackay, "The Starving Time," *National Parks*, November 1998, p. 40.

★ FURTHER READING ★

Aronson, Marc. *Sir Walter Ralegh and the Quest for El Dorado*. New York: Clarion Books, 2000.

Doherty, Kieran. *Soldiers, Cavaliers, and Planters: Settlers of the Southeastern Colonies*. Minneapolis: Oliver Press, 1999.

Dolan, Edward F. *The Lost Colony of Roanoke*. New York: Benchmark Books, 2002.

Hubbard-Brown, Janet. *A History Mystery: The Secret of Roanoke Island*. New York: Morrow Avon, 1991.

Longmeyer, Carole M., ed. *Croatoan*. Peachtree City, Georgia: Gallopade International, 1994.

Schouweiler, Thomas. *The Lost Colony of Roanoke: Opposing Viewpoints*. San Diego: Greenhaven Press Inc, 1991.

Shirley, John W. *Sir Walter Ralegh and the New World*. Raleigh, North Carolina: North Carolina Archives, 1997.

★ Internet Addresses ★

Davenport Public Library. "History in Depth: The Lost Colony of Roanoke." *The Reference Desk: History*. © 1998. <http://www.rbls.lib.il.us/dpl/ref/histhidlost.htm>.

Kid Info. "The Roanoke Colony." *Reference Resources*. n.d. <http://www.kidinfo.com/American_History/Colonization_Roanoke.html>.

National Parks Service. "The Search for the Lost Colony—Fort Raleigh National Historic Site." *Roanoke Revisited: Heritage Education Program*. n.d. <www.nps.gov/fora/search.htm>.

★ Index ★